chess software
user's guide

Byron Jacobs

Jacob Aagaard

John Emms

EVERYMAN CHESS

Gloucester Publishers plc   www.everymanchess.com

First published in 2003 by Gloucester Publishers plc (formerly Everyman Publishers plc), Gloucester Mansions, 140A Shaftesbury Avenue, London WC2H 8HD

British Library Cataloguing-in-Publication Data
A catalogue record for this book is available from the British Library.

ISBN 1 85744 284 9

Distributed in North America by The Globe Pequot Press, P.O Box 480, 246 Goose Lane, Guilford, CT 06437-0480.

All other sales enquiries should be directed to Everyman Chess, Gloucester Publishers plc, Gloucester Mansions, 140A Shaftesbury Avenue, London WC2H 8HD
tel: 020 7539 7600 fax: 020 7379 4060
email: info@everymanchess.com
website: www.everymanchess.com

EVERYMAN CHESS SERIES (formerly Cadogan Chess)
Chief advisor: Garry Kasparov
Commissioning editor: Byron Jacobs

Typeset and edited by First Rank Publishing, Brighton.
Cover design by Horatio Monteverde.
Production by Navigator Guides.
Printed and bound in Great Britain by Biddles Ltd.

Contents

Bibliography

Books

Chess on the Net, Crowther (Everyman 2001)

Die EndspielUniversität, Mark Dvoretsky (Chessgate 2002 – to be published in English 2003 from Russell under the name Endgame University)

Domination in 2545 Studies, Kasparjan (Progress Publishers 1980)

Informant 86

Rapid Chess Improvement, Michael De La Maza (Everyman 2002)

Secrets of Practical Chess, John Nunn (Gambit 1998)

The Mammoth Book of Chess, Graham Burgess (Robinson 2000)

Software and CDs

Intensive Tactics Course, George Renko (Chessbase CD)

King's Indian with h3, Martin Breutigam (Chessbase CD)

Big Database 2002 (Chessbase)

Endgame Study Database 2000, Harold Van Der Heijden (Chessbase CD)

Fritz 7 (ChessBase)

Mega Database 2003 (ChessBase)

The Basic Principles of Chess Strategy, Vol. 1-3, A Bartashnikov (Chessbase CD)

CT-ART. 3.0., Blokh: (Chess Assistant CD)

ChessBase 8.0 (ChessBase)

Website

TWIC

Introduction

In 1958, Bobby Fischer became a grandmaster at the age of 15. This was an unprecedented achievement at such a tender age and it was generally assumed that no other player would get remotely close to being able to emulate this feat. For many years, even in the 1970s and 1980s, it was quite common for the holder of the title 'world's youngest grandmaster' to be a highly mature 18 or even 19 year old.

However, in the last ten years, all this has changed. First of all the Hungarian Judit Polgar beat Fischer's record, which had stood for over 30 years, by a couple of months. After that, the floodgates opened: Peter Leko got there at 14, as did Etienne Bacrot, Ruslan Ponomariov and Teimour Radjabov. Then the Chinese player Bu Xiangzhi acquired the title at 13 years and ten months. But even these achievements were dwarfed by the Ukrainian Sergey Karjakin who registered his final grandmaster norm at the truly astonishing age of 12.

I do not think it is a coincidence that these amazing feats have all occurred simultaneously with the recent technological revolution. The last 10-15 years have radically changed the way that chess can now be played and studied. There are three main reasons for this:

1) Almost every remotely serious chessplayer must now be aware that software programs exist that can more or less hold their own even against world champions, as has been witnessed in several matches. Such advances have been made possible by the incredible increases in raw computing power that have occurred. The commercial software packages that are based around these programs are very useful for

players of all strengths from complete beginner to the very best grandmasters. These packages can analyse your play and suggest where you are going wrong. They are also ideal sparring partners, happy to play any kind of position at any time, or to analyse any positions they are given and to present their conclusions. Access to such packages must inevitably speed up the process by which chess knowledge is gained.

2) The internet is a wonderful resource for the keen chessplayer. You can play other players on-line, receive coaching, download the latest games and watch games in major tournament as they happen. This change in access to information is quite astonishing. As recently as 1988, Jon Speelman sprung a new move on Nigel Short in a critical game in their World Championship Quarter-Final Match. In fact the move was not completely new, having been played a couple of weeks previously in a game in the Soviet Championship. The reason that Speelman new about the move and was able to prepare it was that the girlfriend of his second, Jon Tisdall, had noticed the game when it was published in a Norwegian newspaper. This was just 15 years ago but now, in this age of the internet, the fact that an important new move could only be discovered by a strong grandmaster 'en passant' seems rather quaint. Nowadays such a development would be witnessed in real time and would remain secret for approximately one nano-second.

3) Many software houses now produce highly sophisticated packages that can create and manage huge databases of chess information. Most serious players, and even a substantial number of casual enthusiasts, now have such packages. These make it much easier to study openings, middlegames and endgames than ever before.

As with technological developments in all areas of life such advances create their own problems. What is the best way to manage this tsunami of information without becoming completely bewildered and feeling swamped? How best to use chess-playing software? What is the best way to study middlegames and endgames? It is questions such as these that this book will attempt to answer.

The contributions in this book are from two battle-hardened professionals who have been playing, coaching and writing about chess for many years and are hugely experienced at using chess software. The first three chapters were written by the strong grandmaster John Emms, who has both played for and managed the English Olympic squad and is highly regarded as a chess author. Chapters four to six are the work of Danish International Master Jacob Aagaard. Jacob is a leading chess coach with very specific ideas about how chess should be studied and the role that software can play in that process. His book *Excelling at Chess* won the prestigious chesscafe.com Book of the Year Award.

The ideas in this book are mainly illustrated with screenshots that come from ChessBase (database package) and Fritz (playing program). Both of these packages are produced by ChessBase gmbh who are based in Hamburg and are generally regarded as the world leaders in chess software. However, there are many other packages available that will also perform the tasks illustrated here.

Byron Jacobs,
Sussex, August 2003

Chapter One

Managing Databases

For a number of years now serious chess players have recognised the value of using chess database programs to improve their game. Programs such as ChessBase allow the user to store and input large numbers of games, to view these games on a computer screen, to add notes and analysis, and to sort and classify games in a beneficial way. It's clear that chess database programs are a powerful learning and preparation tool for chess players. In my opinion, they are at least partly responsible for the growing number of young world-class players. Twenty years ago it was headline news if a teenager obtained his or her grandmaster title. Nowadays this is par for the course, and the record for the youngest ever grandmaster has been broken numerous times (most recently by a 12-year old Ukrainian, Sergey Karjakin). In the old days an improving player had to rely on over-the-board experience, books and a chess set. Of course there's nothing wrong with this, but it's quite time-consuming leafing through various books to find the right variations, plus continually resetting the pieces and checking you have the right position in front of you. Nowadays chess database programs, together with chess computer engines, have dramatically shortened the learning process. With a few keystrokes, you can master the main ideas in an opening, study the success rates of different variations, perform a deep analysis of your own games, see if a particular position has been reached before, examine the games of prospective opponents, and much more besides.

In this chapter we will be dealing with handling chess databases and creating a database of your own games. In Chapter 2 we move on to the subject of studying the opening with database programs and chess-playing engines. Finally, in Chapter 3, we will look at studying the strengths and weaknesses of your own game and those of prospective opponents.

Creating a Database of your own Games

If you only had limited study time available, or if you were allowed to do just one thing to improve your game, then you should always choose to study and annotate your own games. Each battle you have is a vital learning experience, but the benefits can easily be lost if you choose to ignore the experience. Going through the game with your opponent and/or a coach is obviously beneficial. And once you have collected all the analysis, opening ideas and suggested improvements, it's vital to record the information before you forget anything important. In previous times keen players would jot down their comments on their scoresheet and then transfer these to an exercise book containing neat annotations of their games. Nowadays the answer is simpler. Using a database program, you can create a database of your own games on your computer.

If you have just bought a database program such as ChessBase, you could simply input games you play from now on. However, it is obviously more beneficial to key in games you have played in the past, although I understand that this could be a rather time-consuming job. Say you have played chess seriously for ten years, and you have played an average of forty games per year, then this gives you 400 games to key in. You could probably expect to input around ten to fifteen games per hour. So, depending on your mouse skills, the task would take between 25 and 40 hours. But believe me, it's worth it!

If you have made any notes to these games, then these can be keyed in at the same time. You could also have a chess engine like Fritz running in the background to point out any obvious tactical errors. However, all this stuff can be done at a later date. The main point of the exercise is just to get all your games in.

If you have played in international or important national events, then you could find that some of your games are already available on commercial databases such as ChessBase's Mega Database or Big Database. You could then save some time by copying these games into the appropriate database. However, a word of warning: be careful to check the data with your own scoresheet as mistakes are often made on these commercial databases. Someone else has obviously had to key in your game for the tournament bulletin and, depending on neatness of handwriting, keying in someone else's game can often be a thankless task!

Analysing Your Games with a Chess Engine

Once you have analysed your game, it is certainly worthwhile checking the moves you played and your analysis with a chess engine. If we take Fritz as an example, there are a few options available. One is to have the engine running in the background in ChessBase (or Fritz) as you key in the moves and the analysis of the game. Fritz will soon tell you if you there is something wrong with any of the moves or your analysis. It will guide you through complex variations and make some worthwhile suggestions for both sides. In fact, this is the method that I use. I believe this to be a more thorough choice than those described below, and one that should certainly be used by more experienced players. The reason for this is that you have control of the engine and can guide it to what you believe are the critical positions.

A second option is to perform a **blunder check** in the Fritz program. Here Fritz will go through both the moves of the game and the notes, suggesting alternatives if it believes they are stronger. The following is a slightly edited version of a game that has been through a blunder check. I set the minimum analysis time per move at ten seconds and set a low 'threshold' so that the program would point out small errors as well as blunders.

□ Cicak ■ Emms

Cappelle La Grande 1997

Ruy Lopez

---

1 e4 e5 2 Nf3 Nc6 3 Bb5 a6 4 Ba4 Nf6 5 0-0 b5 6 Bb3 Bc5 7 Nxe5 Nxe5 8 d4 Bxd4 9 Qxd4 d6 10 c3 0-0 11 Bg5 Bb7 12 f3 c5 13 Qd1 h6 14 Bh4

last book move

14...Re8 15 Na3

-0.44 Fritz 7: 15 Nd2 c4 16 Bc2 Ng6 17 Bf2 d5 18 Bd4 dxe4 19 fxe4 0.00/10

15...Ng6 16 Bf2 c4 17 Bc2 d5 18 exd5 Nf4 19 d6 N6d5 20 Re1 Qg5

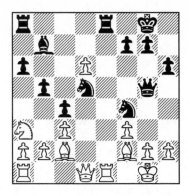

21 g3

-2.44 Fritz 7: 21 Rxe8+ Rxe8 22 Qf1 Bc8 23 Kh1 Re6 24 g3 Nd3 -0.53/9

21...Nh3+ 22 Kf1 Nxf2 23 Kxf2 Ne3 24 Qd4

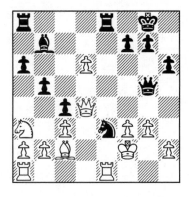

24...Nxc2

-0.37 Fritz 7: 24...Qh5 25 Rxe3 Qxh2+ 26 Kf1 Qh1+ 27 Kf2 Qxa1 28 Re7 Rxe7 29 dxe7 Re8 30 Qd7 -2.44/9

25 Nxc2 Qh5 26 Rxe8+ Rxe8 27 Ne1 Qxh2+ 28 Ng2 Qh5

-0.37 Fritz 7: 28...Bc6 -0.60/10

29 Nh4 Qd5

0.63 Fritz 7: 29...Qg5 30 Rd1 Bc6 31 Qf4 Qxf4 32 gxf4 Bd7 33 f5 Kf8 34 Rd2 a5 35 f6 gxf6 -0.25/11

30 Qxd5 Bxd5 31 a4

0.18 Fritz 7: 31 Nf5 Kf8 32 Ne7 Be6 33 Rd1 0.63/14

31...Be6 32 f4 g6

0.47 Fritz 7: 32...Rd8 33 axb5 axb5 34 Ra6 Bg4 35 Nf3 Bxf3 36 Kxf3 f5 37 g4 fxg4+ 38 Kxg4 g6 39 d7 Rxd7 0.18/13

33 Nf3 bxa4

1.04 Fritz 7: 33...Rd8 34 axb5 axb5 35 Ra6 Kg7 36 Nd4 Kf6 37 Nxb5 Rb8 38 Nd4 Rxb2+ 39 Ke3 Rg2 40 d7 Rxg3+ 0.59/13

34 Rxa4 Rb8 35 Rxa6 Rxb2+ 36 Ke3 Rc2 37 Kd4 Rg2

1.41 Fritz 7: 37...Kg7 38 Ne5 Rd2+ 39 Kc5 g5 40 Ra1 gxf4 41 gxf4 Kf6 42 Rh1 Kg7 43 Rg1+ Kf6 1.06/12

38 Ne5 Rxg3 39 Ra8+ Kg7

40 Re8

0.25 Fritz 7: 40 Nxc4 g5 41 Nb6 Rg1 42 Kc5 Rd1 43 fxg5 1.04/12

40...Rg1 41 Re7

-0.50 Fritz 7: 41 Kc5 Rd1 42 Nf3 Kf6 43 Nd4 h5 44 Nxe6 0.13/12

41...Kf6 42 Nd7+ Bxd7 43 Rxd7 Rd1+ 44 Kc5 g5

0.04 Fritz 7: 44...h5 45 Rd8 Kf5 46 Rf8 Kxf4 47 Kc6 f5 48 d7 g5 49 d8Q Rxd8 50 Rxd8 Kg3 51 Rd4 -0.32/14

45 fxg5+ hxg5 46 Re7 g4 47 Re4 Kf5 48 Rxc4 g3 49 Rd4 Rxd4 50 cxd4 Ke6 51 Kc6 g2 52 d7 g1Q 53 d8Q Qc1+ 54 Kb5 ½-½

I guess a few things should be explained here. The figure immediately after a text move is Fritz's assessment of the position after that move.

It then suggests an improvement and gives a line of analysis. At the end of the analysis Fritz gives an assessment of that final position together with the search depth. Roughly speaking, chess engines equate a one point advantage with being a pawn up (or a three-point advantage with being a minor piece up). Also, positive numbers equate to a white advantage, whereas negative numbers give Black the advantage. So, for example, Fritz assesses the position after 40 Re8 as being 0.25 in White's favour, but White could have reached an advantage of 1.04 with 40 Nxc4.

Using the blunder check we can see how the above game ebbed and flowed. After the opening moves Cicak made the first slight error (15 Na3) before making a serious mistake with 21 g3. I then held a winning advantage for a few moves before blowing this with 24...Nxc2, when 24...Qh5 would have kept the decisive advantage. I continue to make small errors (29...Qd5, 32...g6), which give my opponent some winning chances. However, Cicak returns the compliment on move 40 and after this the game edges towards a draw.

This method is very useful for discovering mistakes in the game or the analysis. Nevertheless, there are certain limitations. Fritz doesn't necessarily have a good eye for critical positions and may easily pass over one, especially if the time allocation per move is insufficient. On the other hand, you don't want Fritz spending fifteen minutes on every move, otherwise the job would never get done. This is why a chess-playing engine is more economical when guided by the user.

In my opinion, the Fritz blunder check is more useful than the **Full analysis** option, whereby Fritz analyses and annotates the game in a more 'user-friendly' way, using verbal explanations rather than just assessments by numbers. However, Fritz only annotates the moves played in the game (it actually deletes the notes), and comes up with some strange explanations (see Figure 1). It looks as if humans have still got the edge when it comes to annotations!

Opening Keys for your Database

Without a doubt, one of the most powerful features of the ChessBase program is the opening key. Games in databases can be automatically classified into different keys depending upon the opening moves. This gives users very quick access to all games arising from the same opening. If you have a certain game loaded in the game window, simply the press of a key (Shift F6) will list all the games that are in the same key, with the nearest match at the top. This, of course, is highly beneficial for the user.

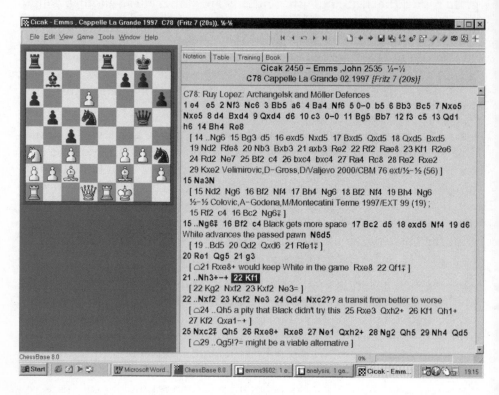

Figure 1

Fritz 8 on 'full analysis' mode

These opening keys can either be very primitive, very refined or somewhere in between. Commercial ChessBase databases such as Mega Database 2002 and Big Database 2002 come with complex keys, while ChessBase 8 offers two different types. The 'big' key is based on the legendary *Encyclopaedia of Chess Openings* (ECO) codes. There are 500 main keys (coded A00-E99) and each of these contain many sub-keys. In all, the 'big' key contains around 55,000 classification positions. This key works well with large databases but is simply too refined for small and medium-sized databases.

The 'small' key has just over 100 classification positions and uses descriptive labels such 'Sicilian Alapin Variation', 'Ruy Lopez/Spanish' and 'Centre Counter/Scandinavian'. Its size dictates that this would be a better choice for a personal games database, but it's certainly not perfect. For example, it fails to recognise many transpositions and misses out popular lines (there is no key for the Sicilian Taimanov – 1 e4 c5 2 Nf3 e6 3 d4 cxd4 4 Nxd4 Nc6).

It's true that it's difficult to construct a perfect opening key which keeps everybody happy, but therein lies the solution – construct your own! Okay, it may take you a few hours and you will still have to deal with lots of transpositional problems, but you only have to concentrate on your own openings, and by the end it's likely that you will have a very solid understanding of the opening keys related to your games.

To give an example I decided to create my own opening keys for a sample database. I created a medium-sized database of my own games from 1996 to the present day. I called the database 'emms9602' and it contains 535 games. Below is a brief explanation of how to create an opening key to suit your needs. (I should admit that in fact I'm reasonably happy with an ECO-based key for my own games database, but this is only because I have years of experience using ECO codes and I'm very familiar with virtually every code connected with my openings.)

The way that opening keys work in ChessBase is that the program plays through each game backwards, looking for classification positions in the opening keys. As soon as it encounters a classification position, it knows immediately to which key the game belongs.

The first classification position that I need is the initial position (no moves by either side). This position represents unusual first moves by White (1 g3, 1 f4 etc.). The first stage is to open a new board window. Naturally I don't need to key in any moves as I already have the initial position in front of me. I now click the openings tab in the list window, insert a new key and type in the name 'others'. I return to the board window and play the move 1 e4. I then go back to the openings tab and insert a new key, calling it '1 e4'. This step is repeated with the initial moves 1 d4, 1 c4 and 1 Nf3. With this completed, it's worth asking the program even at this early stage to classify the whole database using the new keys. The results are seen in Figure 2.

Already we can see some significant findings. There are as many as 389 games in the 1 e4 key (this is an unsurprisingly large number as I virtually always play 1 e4 with White). This key certainly has to be refined a lot further, as does 1 d4 and, to a lesser extent, 1 Nf3 and 1 c4. However, there are only six games in 'others'. With that number of games, this key is easily manageable and, with the exception of possible transpositions, requires no further refining.

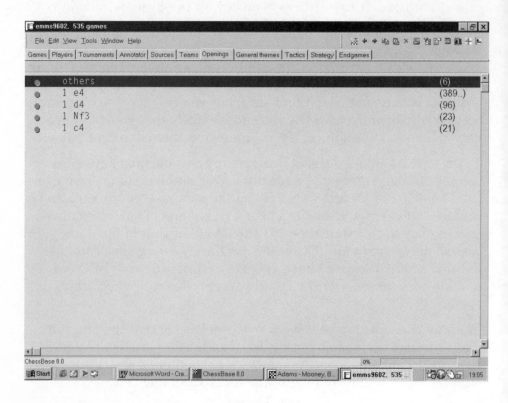

Figure 2

A primitive key

I now go about refining the '1 e4' key by creating a number of sub-keys. I first double-click on '1 e4' in the openings tab. This takes me down a level and lists the 389 games beginning with 1 e4. On a board window I input the moves 1 e4 c5. I go back to the openings tab and insert a new key, calling it '1...c5'. I repeat this process with several other popular replies to 1 e4. I again ask the program to classify the whole database and the results can be seen in Figure 3.

As you can see, the number of games in each key is becoming more manageable, but there is still the need for further refinement, especially with the Sicilian and 1...e5. It depends on an individual's tastes, but I find that if a single key contains ten or less games then there is usually no need for further refinement and the only thing to worry about then are possible transpositions. In this particular case I can leave the keys 1...d5 and 1...Nf6. I should be careful with 1...d6 and 1...g6, as these two moves can easily transpose. It's probably best to refine the 1...d6 key further as the program will automatically spot the transpositions from 1...g6. For example, the position arising after 1 e4 d6 2 d4 Nf6 3 Nc3 g6 4 Nf3 Bg7 occurs seven times in this database, but two of these games began 1 e4 g6. If I add the classification position after 4...Bg7, all seven games will go into that key.

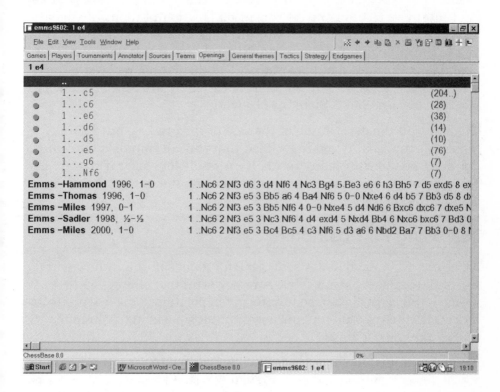

Figure 3

A slightly more refined key

If you look at the bottom of the list in Figure 3, you will spot that five games don't belong in any of the sub-keys. These are 'other replies to 1 e4' and would include moves such as 1...b6, 1...a6, 1...g5 etc. In reality, no one seems to play those moves against me anymore and so we are left with five examples of 1...Nc6. Of course there was a case for including 1...Nc6 as a separate key, but in fact there would eventually only be one game in the 1...Nc6 key. The reason for this is that four of the games begin 1 e4 Nc6 2 Nf3 e5 and these would eventually find their way into a 1 e4 e5 2 Nf3 Nc6 key.

Refining the 1 e4 c5 key presents me with some transpositional problems. For example, I input the classification position after 1 e4 c5 2 c3 and call the sub-key '2 c3'. When I reclassify the games, there are 30 that drop into that key. However, I also notice that there are still a few c3 Sicilians in the 1 e4 c5 key. The reason for this is that c3 Sicilians can also occur with the move orders 2 Nf3 Nc6 3 c3 and 2 Nf3 e6 3 c3. To get around this problem I need to input the classification positions after 2 Nf3 Nc6 3 c3 and 2 Nf3 e6 3 c3 into the '2 c3' key (a key can contain more than one classification position). I input the moves 2 Nf3 Nc6 3 c3 on a board window, right click on the '2 c3' key and choose the option **Define new position**. I repeat this with 2 Nf3 e6 3 c3 and now this key should capture all c3 Sicilians. I reclassify the whole database to check it works. It does! There are now 55 games in the '2 c3' key and no c3 Sicilians elsewhere.

I'll spare you the description of the rest of the process, but I think you've got the idea. If you're worried that this all sounds a bit confusing, don't be. As with many tasks, it's a whole lot easier if you are actually trying it out yourself in front of a computer rather than just reading the theory.

Searching for Positions

We've already talked about searching for games in the same opening key in ChessBase, but an even more powerful tool allows you to search a reference database for any given position. This feature is useful for all kinds of studying purposes, but it's particularly helpful when studying openings.

Say you had just played a game and you wished to see if a particular position has been reached before, then you could simply key in the position in the game window, set your reference database, press Shift F7 and, hey presto, all the relevant games are listed. Figure 4 shows an example of this in ChessBase 8. Taking the position after Black's ninth move in Game 3 of the recent Deep Fritz-Kramnik match, I found that there were sixteen matches in Mega Database 2002 (Figure 4 shows the first twelve – you would have to scroll down for the final four).

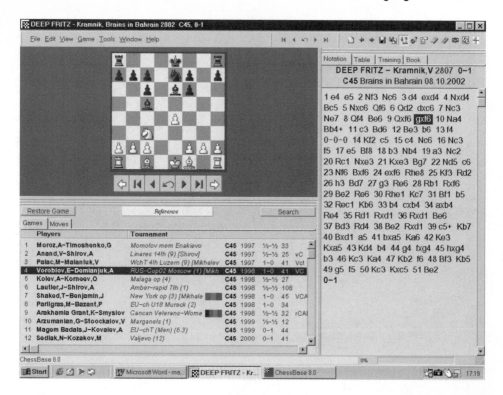

Figure 4

Searching for games with the same position

Of course, having immediate access to these games is a great help if you want to study the position after 9...gxf6. One very useful feature is that you can merge any number of games in the list with the main game. If you wished to merge the game Anand-Shirov, Linares 1997 into the main game, you would press the Alt Key (a quirk of Chess-Base 8 – not pressing this would simply load the Anand-Shirov game when clicked), click on the Anand-Shirov game and drag and drop it into the main notation window. As the Anand-Shirov game contains annotations by Shirov, these would also be merged into the main game.

The more complex way to search for a position in ChessBase is to use the **Search mask** (see Figure 5).

Figure 5

Using the search function to find a specific position

This gives the user options regarding other search criteria as well as the position, including the result, the names of the players, the ratings, the date, piece manoeuvres etc.

The main advantage of searching for a specific position rather than for games in the same opening key is that transpositions will not be missed. Take, for example, the game Kasparov-Ponomariov, Linares 2002, which began **1 e4 e6 2 d4 d5 3 Nc3 dxe4 4 Nxe4 Nd7 5 Nf3 Ngf6 6 Nxf6+ Nxf6 7 c3 c5 8 Ne5!?**. If I search for this position in Mega Database 2002 I find nine other examples, but only two actually arise from the French Defence. Six of the games come from the Sicilian after 1 e4 c5 2 c3 d5 3 exd5 Qxd5 4 d4 e6 5 Nf3 Nf6 6 Na3 Qd8 7 Nc4 Nc6 8 Nce5 Nxe5 9 Nxe5. These examples would be missed if the position after 8 Ne5 was searched only in its opening key. The final game arises from a Caro-Kann: 1 e4 c6 2 Nc3 d5 3 Nf3 dxe4 4 Nxe4 Nd7 5 d4 Ngf6 6 Nxf6+ Nxf6 7 Ne5 e6?! 8 c3 c5. In this final example it is actually White to move instead of Black – ChessBase doesn't distinguish in its searches. Of course the extra move should give White a clear advantage, although this is not exploited in the one example: 9 Bg5 a6 10 Qa4+ Bd7 11 Nxd7 Qxd7 12 Bb5?? Qxb5 0-1. The white player shall remain anonymous!

Large Databases

To make the most out of a database program you should really obtain at least one large database (one with a minimum of 50,000 games) and this should be installed onto your hard disk. A large database with quality games can generally be used as your 'reference database'. This is the standard database that is used for searches, classifications, opening reports etc. So if you are studying one of your own games, you can compare your opening play with that from games in the reference database and you can find out where your game diverged from what has been played previously.

Commercial offerings include ChessBase's Big Database and Mega Database. Big Database 2003, which has just been released onto the market, comes with over 2.3 million games. For more money you can buy Mega Database 2003, which has the same number of games but with over 60,000 annotated by strong chess players, many of whom are grandmasters. The basic package of the latest version of Chess Assistant (Chess Assistant 7) also comes with a database of over 2 million games.

For many years serious chess students relied on the legendary *Chess Informant*, the periodical that has existed since 1966. For a long time it was biannual but more recently it has been published three times a year. Chess Informants are bulky books of games annotated by the world's top players and are a must-have for chess professionals. The bookcases in my study are dominated by Chess Informants (so far 85 have been published), but now there is a saner option for those lacking in shelf space. The first 75 editions can now be purchased in a format recognised by most chess database programs, while number 76 onwards can be read on a relatively new program called Chess Informant Reader, which can be downloaded from the Chess Informant website (http://www.sahovski.com/default.htm). Chess Informant Reader is in some ways similar to ChessBase and Chess Assistant, the major limitation being that, as the name suggests, you can only view games, you can't edit or annotate them.

The sister publication of *Chess Informant* is the equally famous *Encyclopaedia of Chess Openings (ECO)*, five mammoth books of opening theory which are revised periodically. These publications, also indispensable to the chess professional, can now be acquired as software and read on *Chess Informant Reader*. In earlier times professional chess players would travel heavy, sporting bulky suitcases packed with *Informants, ECOs* and written notes. Nowadays there is only the need for a slim computer; this means there is more room for other necessities such as clothes!

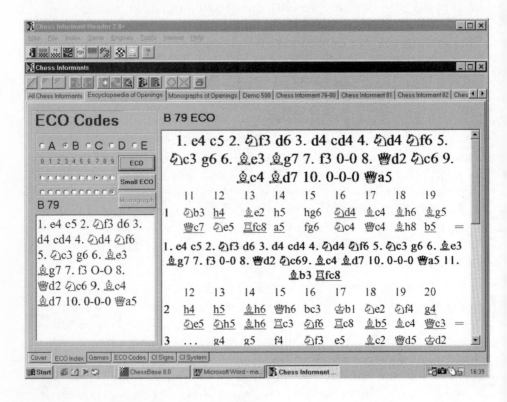

Figure 6

Encyclopaedia of Chess Openings in Chess Informant Reader

Downloading Games from the Net

There are many chess sites where you can download databases of chess games for free, thus providing a useful and up-to-date addition to large databases. Perhaps the most famous chess site that has this feature is Mark Crowther's excellent *The Week in Chess* (http://www.chesscenter.com/twic/twic.html). Crowther started the magazine in September 1994 and since then he's been collecting chess news and game databases which can be downloaded each week. At the time of writing there have been over 420 issues and it's still going as strong as ever. Past issues and databases (from TWIC 211 onwards) can be downloaded from http://www.chesscenter.com/twic/twicp.html, while games from the first 210 issues are available to buy on a CD. Added up, this comes to around 400,000 games. However, the vast majority of these games will already be on ChessBase's Big Database or Mega Database, so if you have one of these it's not really worth your time downloading games from earlier issues of TWIC. Updated versions of Mega Database and Big Database come out every year (Mega Database 2003 has been advertised since November 2002), so the real value of TWIC to serious players is that they can top up their game collection every week from November onwards until a new version of Mega or Big Database is available.

For those keen on acquiring rarer game collections, there are many sites which offer national game databases. For example, Britbase (http://www.bcmchess.co.uk/britbase), which has been put together by *British Chess Magazine* editor John Saunders, is the most comprehensive source of British tournament games available for free download. If you're looking for databases of games played in certain countries or regions, then you could do worse than searching for sites for chess clubs and organisations. A good links page for this can be found at http://www.chesscenter.com/clubs.html.

Handling Different Databases

When I'm studying, preparing for opponents or writing chess books, the chess software I tend to use is ChessBase (for databases), Chess Informant Reader (for viewing ECO and later volumes of Chess Informants), and Fritz (to help with analysis). The main databases I use in ChessBase are Mega Database, TWIC, 'Infobase' (a database of the first 75 Chess Informants), MegaCorr 2 (a database of over 350,000 correspondence games), and 'emmsbase' (a database of my own games).

There are arguments both for and against merging all five of these databases into one gigantic database. I've refrained from doing so but I know that this is how some players prefer to work and it's really down to a matter of taste. Merging all your important databases into one and making that the reference database gives you some obvious advantages:

1) If you are searching for a position, a theme or an openings key, you only need to do this for the one database, thus saving time.

2) Likewise, if you are searching for games from a particular player, you again save time by only needing to use the players' index in the one database.

However, there are also less obvious disadvantages:

1) Your database will be full of game doubles (or even trebles). In ChessBase you have the option of finding and deleting these games, but this can be a cumbersome process when dealing with massive databases and there are still problems at the end. Depending on your settings, many duplicates can remain due to small differences in the game data (see point 2 also). A move missing at the end of one of the versions or a slightly different spelling of player or tournament can be enough for a double to remain. I should say that the doubles remover in ChessBase 8 has improved significantly from previous editions, while it's also not a disaster to have a few doubles floating around. However, those who prefer working with 'pure' databases will want to avoid this.

2) Databases vary somewhat in quality, especially when it comes to consistency in game data. For example, Mega Database, a good quality database, remains consistent when it comes to names of players and tournaments. If you look in the players' index of Mega Database 2002, you will come across only one version of the challenger to Karpov's crown in the late seventies and early eighties. The only listing is Viktor Kortschnoj, and he has 3,886 games to his name. However, other databases of lesser quality may have one or more different spellings. For example, as well as or instead of Viktor Kortschnoj, there could be Kortchnoi or Korchnoi, and Victor or simply V. Merging different databases could well mean that your players' index becomes 'polluted' with different names of the same player. You might wonder what the big deal is, but I'm sure it's annoying to lose a game against Artur Jussupow because you only prepared against Arthur Yusupov!

The method I use, which will be discussed further in Chapters 2 and 3, is to keep the five separate databases and to create smaller specific databases for opening study or for preparing against prospective opponents.

Database Formats

Chess database files come in several different formats. Here's a brief summary of the most important ones.

The ChessBase Format (extension CBH)

The ChessBase format consists of many different files. The extension name of the main file is .cbh, but this file will not work just on its own – there are several other files that are required. If you create a new .cbh file in the later versions of ChessBase (versions 6 onwards), then along with this file the program will create quite a few other files, most of which are vital for the data to be read. This includes extensions such as .cba, .cbc, .cbg, .cbp, .cbs and .cbt. Commercial databases with pre-set keys can have even more files (my Mega Database 2002 has twenty four!). The .cbh format produces powerful indexes and fast searches and also supports a large number of annotation features, including graphic and spoken commentary.

The old ChessBase format, which can still be used in newer programs, has just two crucial files (.cbf and .cbi). A database in the old format can easily be converted to one in the new format by right-clicking the database icon in the database window and choosing 'convert to new format'.

Chess Assistant has a different file format to the ChessBase (.cdp is the main extension and there are several other crucial files). However, Chess Assistant can read .cbh and .cbf files and, crucially, can also handle .pgn files (see below).

If you wish to send a ChessBase file as an attachment to an email, attaching all the relevant files is cumbersome both for the sender and receiver. There are two better alternatives. The first is to simply zip up the relevant files using a zip program such as Winzip (http://www.winzip.com). Another way is to create an archive database (extension .cbv) which will compress all the relevant files into one. This option is also a good way of creating back-up copies of important databases.

Portable Game Notation (extension PGN)

Portable game notation is a very useful text format that can be read by virtually all chess software, which will also generally offer to convert pgn files into their own format.

PGN is very popular for email and the Internet. If you download a chess database from the Internet the chances are that it will be in pgn format. If you wish to send a database file as an attachment on an email, then pgn is a good choice because, compared with the Chess-Base format, there is only one file to download.

PGN files can also be read in any text editor or word processor. Here's how a game, taken from *The Week in Chess*, can look in pgn format.

[Event 'Essent Crown']

[Site 'Hoogeveen NED']

[Date '2002.10.19']

[Round '6']

[White 'Van Wely, L.']

[Black 'Acs, P.']

[Result '0-1']

[ECO 'E48']

[WhiteElo '2681']

[BlackElo '2591']

[PlyCount '36']

[EventDate '2002.10.13']

[Source 'Mark Crowther']

[SourceDate '2002.10.21']

1. d4 Nf6 2. c4 e6 3. Nc3 Bb4 4. e3 O-O 5. Bd3 d5 6. cxd5 exd5 7. Nge2 Re8 8. O-O Bd6 9. a3 Ng4 10. h3 Nh2 11. Re1 Nf3+ 12. gxf3 Qg5+ 13. Kh1 Qh4 14. Nf4 Bxh3 15. Ncxd5 Re6 16. Nxe6 Bf5+ 17. Kg1 Qh2+ 18. Kf1 Bg3 0-1

Sometimes it can be useful to check and edit pgn files manually in word processors. For example, if you annotate games in ChessBase, there is no spell check available, but the spelling in the pgn file can easily be checked in a word-processing program.

Chapter Two

Learning a New Opening

How can you make the most of chess software when you are studying an opening, especially one from scratch? Chess software offers numerous possibilities and mountains of information, so much so that it can seem bewildering at times. There's no doubt that it's useful to have an author guiding you through the opening moves, outlining the main lines and the important tactics and strategies for both sides. Books certainly have an important role to play in this, but there are also many resources to be found in chess software.

Perhaps the easiest way to discover the possibilities with chess software is to select a certain opening and take it from there. Say I want to add the Alekhine Defence (1 e4 Nf6) to my black repertoire and I have ChessBase 8 and Fritz 7 to help. I can't deny that a good book on the subject would be useful, but whereas before this would be the only solution, now it qualifies more as an option rather than a necessity.

Creating a Database

The first task is to create a database of Alekhine Defence games from my major databases. The main advantage of having a reference database full of only Alekhine games is that it will dramatically reduce the time for searches of positions, players, motifs etc. Instead of over 2 million games, we will be dealing with 'only' 30-40 thousand.

As I pointed out in Chapter 1, at the moment I have five main databases: Mega Database 2002, Infobase 1-75, TWIC 1-421, Mega Corr 2 and Emmsbase.

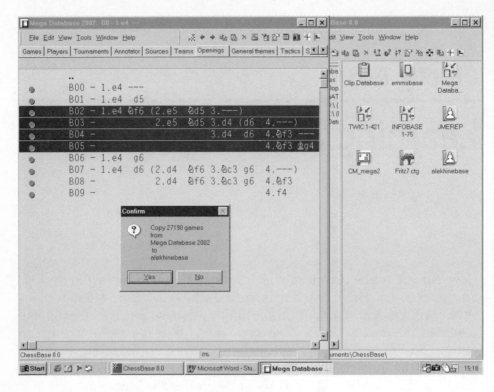

Figure 7

Copying games in opening keys to another database

The first step is to fish out all the Alekhine Defence games from these databases and to lump them into one database that I have imaginatively called alekhinebase. As Mega Database 2002 is by far my biggest database (it contains just over 2 million games), it seems logical to start with this. The way to ensure that I will retrieve all games in the Alekhine Defence is to use the ready-made opening keys. Even with no experience with ECO codes, it doesn't take very long to work out that the Alekhine comes under the codes B02-B05. I highlight these keys, have both the key window and the database window open at the same time (using, for example **Top 2-Vertical** in the Window menu). I then drag and drop games from the highlighted keys into alekhinebase (see Figure 7). There are 27,190 games to copy, some of which are annotated. I have now retrieved all the relevant games from Mega Database 2002, just over one percent of the total games of that database.

Next we repeat this process with all the other databases. Here's a list of the other databases with the number of Alekhine Defence games in brackets: TWIC 1-421 (4,220), Infobase 1-75 (874), Mega Corr 2 (5,486), Emmsbase (18). With this, I now have 37,788 games and all the information required for a substantial base on the Alekhine.

Getting Rid of Doubles

The database of Alekhine Defence games isn't quite the finished product yet. By importing many games from different sources, I have created a substantial number of game doubles. Keeping them in would result in superfluous games, slow down searches and skew statistics, so most should be eliminated. Some doubles, however, should be kept. For example, if a game is annotated both in Mega Database 2002 and Infobase 1-75, then it's logical to keep both games and compare notes. ChessBase 8 also offers the option of merging these games, highlighting the different annotators' contributions to avoid confusion.

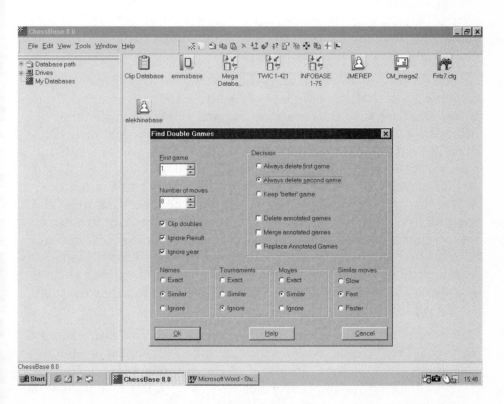

Figure 8

Finding game doubles

To find the doubles I go to **Tools-Database-Find Double Games**. As I mentioned in Chapter 1, ChessBase 8 is much quicker at finding doubles than previous versions, and in under a minute 3,837 doubles are discovered. These games are physically removed from the database with the command **Tools-Database-Remove Deleted Games**. This process takes a minute or so and I'm left with a database of 33,951 Alekhine Defence games, taking up just over eight megabytes of disk space.

Opening Books

An opening book (or tree, as it's sometimes called) is a database of positions rather than games, and in ChessBase it has the extension .ctg. Opening books are very powerful tools for opening study. Using opening books you can discover all the moves that have been played from a given position, the number of times a certain move or position has occurred, the score that move has made and even the rating performance of players who played the move in question. Another advantage is that the problem of move orders is eliminated – the move order to reach a certain position is not relevant.

Given all these positive features, the next logical step is to create an openings book from my database of Alekhine Defence games. I create a new database with the extension .ctg and I name this alekhinebook. I then drag and drop the alekhinebase icon onto the alekhinebook icon. The data from alekhinebase is copied and the tree is created. I have an option to set the absolute length of the tree and I set this to 40 half-moves (20 moves for either side). The longer this is set, the deeper into the position the tree will go, but the more disk space the tree will take up. The Alekhine Defence isn't overly theoretical so I believe that 20 moves should be more than enough. Another option here is to set the **Length after ECO** (or **Relative length**). This length could be set to, say, 20 half-moves after ECO reaches an assessment. This cuts down on overly long branches in rare variations while keeping sufficient depth in important lines.

One word of warning – an opening book does take up a fair amount of disk space. My opening book on the Alekhine Defence takes up 62 megabytes. This amount of space is already quite substantial, especially compared with the eight megabytes needed for the database of games. You can imagine, however, how much disk space would be needed to create a tree from, say, two million games! Fortunately, ChessBase has a way to get over this problem. You can create a temporary opening book by simply selecting all the games in a given database and choosing the option **Games to book**. After closing this temporary book or when leaving the program, the files for the book are deleted from the hard disk.

As I've already mentioned, opening books are useful in many ways. One of the first things you can do if you're not very familiar with the opening in question is to discover what the main lines are simply by browsing through the tree.

Looking at the Alekhine Defence book from the first move I discover that 99 percent of the games in the database begin with 1 e4. But why 'only' 99 percent? What happens with the other one percent? White's other choices are 1 Nc3, 1 Nf3, 1 d3 and even 1 d4. These opening moves, however, can all transpose into lines of the Alekhine. One obvious example is 1 Nc3 d5 2 e4 Nf6, while 1 d3 Nf6 2 e4 is also classified as an Alekhine. Going on to Black's first move after 1 e4, I see that 95 percent of the games continue 1...Nf6, but there are also examples of 1...d5, 1...Nc6, 1...e5, 1...c5, 1...e6, 1...g6, 1...c6 and 1...d6. Believe me, all of these moves can transpose into the Alekhine – I've got the tree to prove it! Here we see an advantage of using ECO opening keys to create opening databases. If I had simply searched for the position after 1 e4 Nf6 in my large databases, I would have missed out on five percent of the games. There is, however, a disadvantage of using ECO codes and I will explain this a bit later.

Now let's see what happens if I keep following the 'main line'. On White's second move, 2 e5 is by far the most popular choice, occurring 80% of the time, while 2 Nc3 is White second choice. Black's overwhelmingly popular reply to 2 e5 is 2...Nd5, against which White normally plays 3 d4 (although 3 c4 is played fifteen percent of the time). After 3 d4 Black virtually always plays 3...d6. The spread of moves after 3...d6 is shown in Figure 9.

White's main choice here is 4 Nf3, which occurs 12,477 times. White scores 58 percent with this move (the average score by White in the Alekhine is 54 percent). The average rating of those playing 4 Nf3 in the database is 2317, and with this move they are performing at 2362. So overall we can see that 4 Nf3 is the most popular move, it's generally the choice of the stronger players and, out of the five most popular selections, it's the most successful move both in scoring percentage and performance over rating.

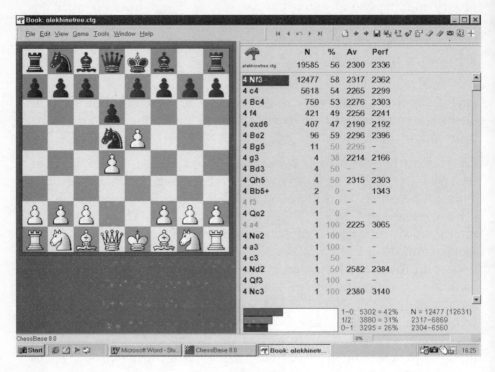

Figure 9

An opening book (or tree)

If we continue down the line of selecting the most popular move at every branch we reach, we end up with the following variation:

1 e4 Nf6 2 e5 Nd5 3 d4 d6 4 Nf3 Bg4 5 Be2 e6 6 0-0 Be7 7 c4 Nb6 8 Nc3 0-0 9 Be3

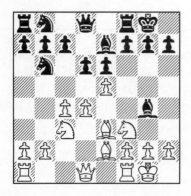

Logically enough, this happens to be one of the main lines of the Alekhine and occurs 786 times on my database.

Now let's see what happens if I choose the second most popular choice for White at move four, then followed by the most popular moves:

1 e4 Nf6 2 e5 Nd5 3 d4 d6 4 c4 Nb6 5 exd6 cxd6 6 Nc3 g6 7 Be3 Bg7 8 Rc1 0-0 9 b3

We have arrived at another main line of the Alekhine Defence, one that occurs over 300 times on my database. The statistics tell me that Black has not scored that well from this position. This can mean a number of things – it doesn't necessarily mean that the position is definitely bad for Black. It might just be that in practice Black has not played the best moves from this position and that the correct way to play has not been found yet. This is something for the prospective Alekhine Defence player to investigate.

If, after some serious study, it is decided that the previous line is unsatisfactory for Black, then attention must turn elsewhere for a suitable line to play. But first of all, let's try another search. What happens when we take only games played between stronger players? Using the search facility, I look for Alekhine Defence games between players who are both over the rating of 2400. I find 2,014 examples, which I select before choosing the option **Games to book**. Having created a temporary tree, I repeat the processes above. As it turns out, the 'main line' is still 1 e4 Nf6 2 e5 Nd5 3 d4 d6 4 Nf3 Bg4 5 Be2 e6 6 0-0 Be7 7 c4 Nb6 8 Nc3 0-0 9 Be3. But what happens if I choose the second most popular choice for White at move four? Then we get the variation

1 e4 Nf6 2 e5 Nd5 3 d4 d6 4 c4 Nb6 5 exd6 exd6 6 Nc3 Be7 7 h3

0-0 8 Nf3 Bf5 9 Be2 Bf6

So, whereas in the main Alekhine Defence database 5...cxd6 is much more popular than 5...exd6 (2,328 games as opposed to 1,464), when you take just the games between stronger players the situation is reversed (141 examples of 5...exd6 compared to 95 examples of 5...cxd6). Again any number of conclusions can be drawn from that, but one thing is clear – it's certainly worthwhile investigating 5...exd6 further.

Other stipulations can be put on searches in order to glean more useful information. Say, for example, that I wished to find out which lines in the Alekhine were currently fashionable amongst the world's elite players. Again using the search facility in my Alekhine database, I look for games played between players over the rating of 2400 in the year 2002. This search reveals 114 games and the most popular line being 1 e4 Nf6 2 e5 Nd5 3 d4 d6 4 Nf3 dxe5 5 Nxe5 c6!?. This variation has hardly featured in the past but it must have some value if all these Grandmasters are starting to play it, and this line is certainly worth some investigation for would-be Alekhine players. It just goes to show that the so-called main lines are not necessarily the best lines.

I have found one limitation to ChessBase's search facility. You can look for games where both players are in a certain rating band, where neither player is, or where at least one player is, or where the average of the two players is. However, you cannot search for games where a specific colour is between the rating bands. This would be useful for finding games where those playing black are, say, over 2400 and the ratings of the white players are irrelevant. You can get around this problem by searching for all games where at least one player is over

2400 and then sorting the resulting list by **Elo Black**. In this case, all the games where the black player is over 2400 would go to the top of the list.

One thing I've noticed when dealing with trees in ChessBase is the strange annotations. For example, in the Alekhine tree the move 1 e4 is adorned with an exclamation mark, while in the line mentioned just now 5...exd6 is rewarded with '!?' and 5...cxd6 gets also gets an exclamation mark! My advice to readers is to simply ignore these signs.

I mentioned a bit earlier that there is one disadvantage with using ECO codes to create a database. If I follow the tree through the moves 1 e4 Nf6 2 Nc3, I notice that there are absolutely no examples of 2...e5, even though it's a perfectly logical move and is played about twenty percent of the time from this position. The problem is that we have transposed into an entirely different opening – the Vienna Game – which normally arises from the move order 1 e4 e5 2 Nc3 Nf6. Should Black wish to play this move then he would have to create another database for the Vienna, which happens to be ECO-coded C26-C29. Another example arises after the moves 1 e4 Nf6 2 Nc3 d5 3 e5 Nfd7 4 d4. In this case the fact that there are no examples of the natural-looking 4...e6 should arouse suspicions. In fact 4...e6 is played about 40 percent of the time and transposes into a well-known line of the French (1 e4 e6 2 d4 d5 3 Nc3 Nf6 4 e5 Nfd7). Again, if Black wished to incorporate this into his repertoire he would need to create a fresh database for this (ECO code C11).

Opening Keys

Despite the enormous benefits of using trees, it's certainly also worthwhile having an opening key. With a database of nearly 34,000 games (all on the Alekhine Defence), the easiest solution is simply to utilise the 'big key' offered by ChessBase 8 (in earlier versions of ChessBase you would have to copy the key from, say, MegaBase). Creating your own key is possible but, unlike with a personal database, with so many games and only one opening it would take a long time and a lot of hard work to refine it properly.

Once you have the keys in place and you have made alekhinebase the reference database, you are able to use the feature **Find novelty** (Shift F6), which will list the games in the same key with the nearest match at the top.

Opening Report

ChessBase (from version 7 onwards) possesses one of the most effective instruments for opening study, one that is also very easy to use; this function is called 'opening report'. At a keystroke, a comprehensive account can be generated on any critical position in a specific opening, using the games in the reference database. This report includes:

1) The earliest and latest games stemming from the position in question.

2) A list of notable players who have used the variation and their success rates.

3) Statistics showing how each side is scoring, the percentage of decisive games and the average length of the games.

4) The most popular moves and plans from the given position, along with the critical lines, the names of the players who have played in this fashion, the scores and the rating performances.

As a practical example, I'll try using an opening report on the Alekhine Defence. We've already discovered by using the opening book that one of the main lines of the Alekhine is **1 e4 Nf6 2 e5 Nd5 3 d4 d6 4 Nf3 Bg4 5 Be2 e6 6 0-0 Be7 7 c4 Nb6 8 Nc3 0-0 9 Be3**. Figure 10 shows a screen shot of the opening book after 9 Be3.

As you can see, the main move for Black in this position is 9...d5. However, say I am looking for an alternative way to play the position and I choose to investigate 9...a5. One point of this move is that Black now has the idea of playing 10...Bxf3! 11 Bxf3 Nxc4 because after 12 Bxb7 the rook has the a7-square at its disposal. Another idea is that after ...d6-d5, c4-c5, ...N6d7 (or ...Nc8), White will not be able to support his c5-pawn with a quick b2-b4.

Some information can be gathered from the opening book. Figure 10 shows some statistics on this move (91 games with Black scoring 45 percent). By clicking on the move 9...a5, I can discover what White's main replies are (10 b3 and 10 exd6 are the leading candidates). To collect more information, I set alekhinebase as my reference database and go to **Tools-Opening Report**.

The history section of the report tells me that the earliest game in the database with 9...a5 was the game Bjelajac-Kovacevic, Zagreb 1977. The report also tells me that, relative to the number of games in each year of the database, 9...a5 was played quite a few times in the years 1985-1990 but has reduced in popularity since then.

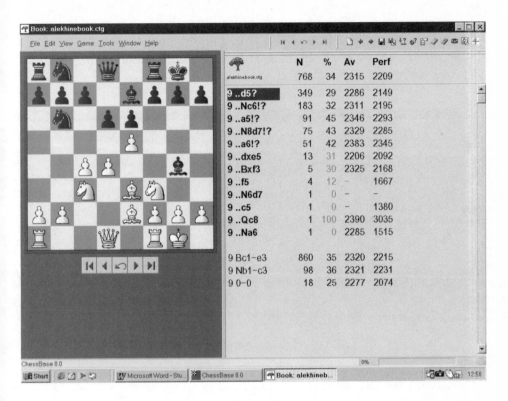

Figure 10

An opening tree listing ninth move options for Black

According to the opening report, 'strong grandmasters' that have used this line as Black include Vlatko Kovacevic, Alex Yermolinsky, Vlastimil Hort, Lembit Oll and Larry Christiansen. 'Other notable players' include Vladimir Bagirov, Lev Alburt and Alexander Shabalov. It goes without saying that the prospective 9...a5 player would do well to study the games of these experts.

I should point something out here. ChessBase bases the distinction between the two categories on the average rating of the player when the games were played. So although Shabalov is now a strong GM with a rating of over 2600, he 'only' counts as a 'notable player' here as one of his games was played in 1988, when his rating was 2430.

The fourth part of the opening report concentrates on possible white replies to 9...a5. The most popular move is the natural 10 b3, covering the c4-pawn and thus dealing with the 'threat' of ...Bxf3. Figure 11 shows this particular section of the report. In reply to 10 b3, Chess-Base states that 'You should play 10...d5.' This is not the result of any analysis on the position by the program, but simply a conclusion drawn from statistics. Because of this, players should be very wary of believing that this is gospel, especially if the conclusion is only based on very few games.

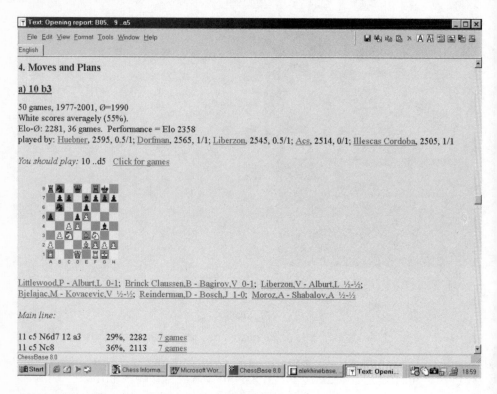

Figure 11

Part of an opening report

The report goes on to state that the main lines are 11 c5 N6d7 12 a3 and 11 c5 Nc8, and follows this up with some plans for both White and Black. In my experience, these plans often look a little jumbled because in many cases it's hard to articulate a plan for one side without taking the opponent's moves into consideration. However, these plans are always accompanied by a link to the relevant games, which should clarify matters. For example, the first plan given for Black is:

Nb6-d7/f7-f6/Be7xf6/Bg4xf3/c7-c6/Nb8-a6/e6-e5/e5xd4

This is accompanied by a link to the following games, which illustrate a successful strategy on Black's part.

□ **P.Littlewood** ■ **Alburt**

Hastings 1981

Alekhine Defence

1 e4 Nf6 2 e5 Nd5 3 d4 d6 4 Nf3 Bg4 5 Be2 e6 6 0-0 Be7 7 c4 Nb6 8 Nc3 0-0 9 Be3 a5 10 b3 d5 11 c5 N6d7 12 a3

ECO prefers 12 Ne1, which is probably a bit better for White.

12...f6 13 exf6 Bxf6 14 Qd2 Bxf3 15 Bxf3 c6 16 Rad1 Na6 17 Bg4 e5 18 Na4 exd4 19 Bxd4 Bxd4 20 Qxd4

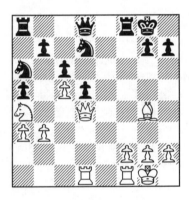

20...Nf6 21 Be6+ Kh8 22 Rfe1 Qc7 23 Bf5 Qf7 24 f3 Nc7 25 Nb6 Rad8 26 a4 Na6 27 Nc4 Ng8 28 Be6 Qf6 29 Nd6 Qxd4+ 30 Rxd4 Nxc5 31 Nf7+ Rxf7 32 Bxf7 Nh6 33 Be8 Nf5 34 Rdd1 g6 35 Bf7 Nxb3

and Black went on to win this favourable endgame.

□ **Brinck Claussen** ■ **Bagirov**

Copenhagen 1993

Alekhine Defence

(up to Black's 20th the game follows Littlewood-Alburt)

20...Rb8 21 Rd3 Nf6 22 Rh3 Qc7 23 Be6+ Kh8 24 Bf5 Rbe8 25 f4 Kg8 26 Nc3 Qe7 27 b4 axb4 28 axb4 Nc7 29 Bd3 Rf7 30 f5 Qe5 31 Ne2 Qxd4+ 32 Nxd4 Rfe7 33 b5 cxb5 34 Nxb5 Nxb5 35 Bxb5 Rc8 36 Rc1 Rec7 37 Ra3 Rxc5 38 Rxc5 Rxc5

and Black eventually converted his extra pawn.

Once (or perhaps if!) you become satisfied with Black's position after 10 b3 d5, the next step would be to study games where White tries different ideas on move ten, including 10 cxd6 and 10 Nd2. With this completed, the prospective Alekhine Defence player will be some way to acquiring a repertoire based on the main line (4 Nf3 Bg4).

It certainly makes sense to study the main lines first as these will amount to a large percentage of what you get in practical games. In the case of the Alekhine Defence, the main lines include 4 Nf3, 4 c4 Nb6 5 exd6 (the Exchange Variation) and 4 c4 Nb6 5 f4 (the Four Pawns Attack). Even without any previous knowledge of the Alekhine, it's easy to work this out from the opening tree. More unusual lines for White (for example 3 c4 Nb6 4 c5) can always be learnt at a later date.

Practice

From my experience, I've found it very difficult to learn openings properly without first having some practical experience in them. In theory it should be possible to study the main ideas and memorise the tricky variations without playing them over the board, but in reality most players find life much easier once they have had a chance to try their new opening a few times in real games. Simply speaking, the lessons learnt over the chessboard are always likely to stick in the memory more than ones learnt from studying books or with a computer.

In most cases it's pretty obvious that there will be some difficult moments and possible defeats when you first start using your new opening, but you would expect this as much as you would expect your results to slowly improve as you gain more experience. Unless you're not worried at all about going straight into the deep end by playing your new opening in competitive games, the sensible thing to do is to build up some experience in 'friendly games'. I can think of three possible ways to do this: playing against a training partner, playing opponents on the Internet, or playing a chess program like Fritz.

The first of these options is, in my opinion, the most beneficial one, but it is also the most difficult to arrange. If you are lucky enough to have a regular sparring partner, then this can be a big help when learning new openings. I would recommend playing lots of rapidplay or blitz games in the same opening line in order to build up familiarity. It's also worth briefly going through each game afterwards to identify the critical points in the opening.

The rate of play in these games can vary according to taste. Personally, I think that anything under five minutes per player is a bit pointless – there is simply not enough time to think of any useful plans. But anything between five and thirty minutes per player will be beneficial and will allow for a reasonable number of games per training session.

Playing opponents on the Internet is in some ways less useful for learning a specific new opening because you cannot determine what your opponents are going to play. If you wanted to practise playing the Alekhine Defence, you would probably only get it around 20 percent of the time because around half your games would be as White, while as Black you would also face 1 d4, 1 c4 etc. On the other hand, one advantage is that the number of different styles from opponents would lead to a greater variety of experience.

Playing against a chess-playing program such as Fritz naturally gives you more control over the opening moves and time limits. Against Fritz, the simple way of ensuring you get the right opening is to put the machine into a non-playing mode (**Infinite analysis**) and then just play the opening moves for both sides until you reach the desired position. At this point you can start the game by prompting Fritz to move.

It's also a good idea to load an openings book (Fritz plays some unusual lines when left to its own devices including, at blitz chess, 1 e4 e5 2 Nf3 Nf6 3 Nxe5 Qe7!?). To gain some practice with the main line of the Alekhine Defence, I loaded the previously created alekhine-book.ctg into Fritz and then edited the book to encourage Fritz to play the lines I wanted practice against. After our first encounter (played at a time limit of four minutes each plus an additional two seconds per move), I briefly studied the game with the help of Fritz and ChessBase and made some notes on the important points which I could refer to at a later date. This is a slightly edited result.

□ **Fritz 7** ■ **Emms**

Kent 2003

Alekhine Defence

1 e4 Nf6 2 e5 Nd5 3 d4 d6 4 Nf3 Bg4 5 Be2 e6 6 0-0 Be7 7 c4 Nb6 8 Nc3 0-0 9 Be3 a5 10 b3 d5 11 c5 N6d7 12 Rc1

12...c6

The other pawn break is 12...f6!? 13 exf6 Bxf6 14 Qd2 c6 (14...Nc6?! allows a trick: 15 Ng5! Bxe2 16 Nxe6 Qe8 17 Nxf8 Bxf1 18 Nxd7 Qxd7 19 Rxf1 and White is a clear pawn ahead) 15 Rfe1 and White is probably slightly better.

13 Qd2

13 Nd2 Bxe2 14 Qxe2 f6! (14...b6 15 cxb6 Qxb6 16 Qg4 Kh8 17 Nf3 Na6 18 Bg5 was good for White in Mainka-J.Graf, Germany 1991) 15 exf6 Bxf6 16 f4 Na6 looks okay for Black.

13...b6 14 cxb6 Nxb6 15 Rfd1 N8d7 16 Nb1 Qc7

This is fine but Black can avoid White's next move with 16...Bxf3, after which 17 Bxf3 Qc7 18 Be2 Rfc8 looks equal.

17 Bg5 Bxg5 18 Nxg5 Bxe2 19 Qxe2 h6 20 Nf3 a4!? 21 b4 Nc4 22 Nfd2 Ndb6 23 Nxc4 Nxc4 24 Nd2 Nb2 25 Re1

25...Qb6?

25...a3! keeps equality, as 26 b5 can be answered by 26...Qb6! 27 bxc6 Rfc8.

26 a3! Rfc8?! 27 Rc2 Nc4 28 Nxc4 dxc4 29 Rxc4 Rd8 30 Qg4 Rd5 31 Recl Rc8 32 h3 Rcd8? 33 Rxc6 Qxd4 34 Qxd4 Rxd4 35 Ra6 Rd2 36 Rxa4 1-0

In our second game Fritz plays the theoretically recommended line according to *ECO* and my lack of experience with the opening shows quite clearly.

□ **Fritz 7** ■ **Emms**

Kent 2003

Alekhine Defence

---

1 e4 Nf6 2 e5 Nd5 3 d4 d6 4 Nf3 Bg4 5 Be2 e6 6 0-0 Be7 7 c4 Nb6 8 Nc3 0-0 9 Be3 a5 10 b3 d5 11 c5 N6d7 12 Nel! Bxe2 13 Qxe2

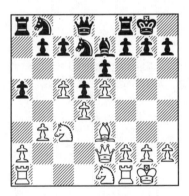

13...c6?!

This is too slow. Black must make a pawn break immediately.

a) 13...f6 looks too weakening on this occasion: 14 exf6 Bxf6 15 Nd3, when White's knight is well placed and he will follow up with Qg4.

b) 13...b6! looks right: 14 cxb6 Nxb6 (14...c5 15 Na4 cxd4 16 Bxd4 Nc6 17 Nf3 Qb8 18 Rac1 Rc8 19 Qb5 was clearly better for White in Illescas Cordoba-Fernandez Aguado, Santa Catalina 1987) 15 Nd3! (15 Qc2?! Na6 16 Nd3 Qd7 17 a3 Rfc8 18 Nc5 Qc6 19 Nxa6 Rxa6 20 Qd3 Qb7 21 f4 c5 22 dxc5 Nd7 23 Na4 Nxc5 24 Nxc5 Bxc5 25 Bxc5 Rxc5 was better for Black in Bjelajac-Kovacevic, Zagreb 1977, while 15 f4 g6! 16 Nd3 Na6 looks OK – Fernandez Garcia) 15...Na6 16 Rac1 Qd7 (16...Qb8? 17 Qg4 Kh8 18 Bg5 was dangerous for Black in Rhodin-Grosse Kloenne, Germany 1990) 17 Qg4 Rfc8! 18 Nc5 Qe8 and White is slightly better, but Black's position is still very playable.

14 Qg4! g6 15 Nf3 b6 16 cxb6 Nxb6 17 Ne2 N8d7 18 Rac1 Rc8 19 Bh6 Re8 20 Rfd1 c5 21 dxc5 Nxc5 22 Ned4 Qd7 23 Ng5 Bd8 24 Qh3 Na6 25 Ngf3 Nb4 26 Rxc8 Qxc8? 27 a3 Na6 28 Bg5 Qd7 29 Qh6 1-0

Two games and two defeats, but these were hardly painful as I was up against, at blitz level, a 2800 monster. The crucial aspect is that I have gained valuable and recorded experience in one of the main lines of the Alekhine Defence. A few games like this followed by employing the same routines with the Exchange Variation and the Four Pawns Attack would leave me in a good position to try out the Alekhine in competitive games.

One final thing is that you can, of course, tailor Fritz's playing strength to suit your own needs. On this occasion I had Fritz playing at the highest level, but by using the handicap mode you can adjust the playing level to one you are more likely to meet in practical play.

Repertoire Database

One further feature of ChessBase is the repertoire database, in which you have the opportunity to collect and maintain games or variations of your opening repertoire. This is particularly useful for accessing relevant games in your repertoire from brand new databases (the latest TWIC etc.).

First I create a new database, which I call 'emmsrepertoire'. Then I go into the properties section of the database (right-click on database icon and choose 'properties') and click the option 'repertoire database'. The database is now ready to receive games and variations.

The next step is to start filling the repertoire database with my openings. Assuming I want to play the Alekhine Defence, I open a new board window, insert the moves 1 e4 Nf6, right-click on the board (this right-click feature is very useful) and choose the option **Add to repertoire**. ChessBase then gives me the option of saving the variation into the repertoire database. I edit the data to simply say 'Alekhine Defence' and click the **OK** button. To check everything has worked, I now double-click the repertoire database and see that the games list has one entry – Alekhine Defence. I double-click on this and a board window comes up (see Figure12). Everything looks okay.

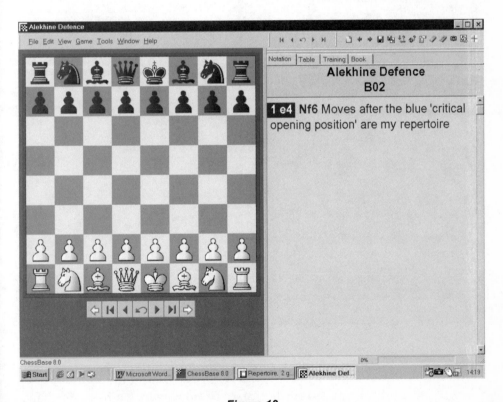

Figure 12

A game in a repertoire database

Now let's see how this can benefit me. I've just downloaded the latest TWIC (TWIC 426) and wish to look at all the Alekhine games. With the repertoire database, I now have the option of using the search function for TWIC 426 and clicking the option **In repertoire** in the **Game data** tab. The result is a list of seven Alekhine Games from TWIC 426.

Now let's try something slightly more complex that highlights a glitch in ChessBase 8, one that doesn't exist in earlier versions. In the highly popular Sveshnikov Sicilian, I play the line **1 e4 c5 2 Nf3 Nc6 3 d4 cxd4 4 Nxd4 Nf6 5 Nc3 e5 6 Ndb5 d6 7 Bg5 a6 8 Na3 b5 9 Nd5** as White. It would be useful to be able to check new databases for this position, so I go through the procedure described above. However, when I check to see if everything is okay, I end up with the following game window (see Figure 13)

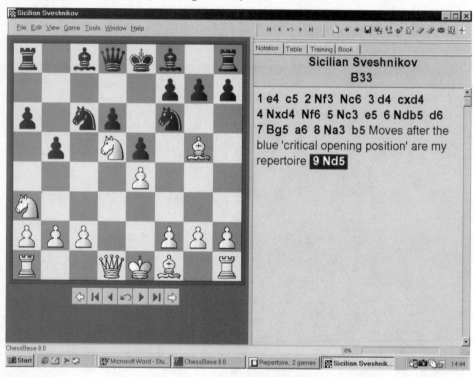

Figure 13

A problem with ChessBase 8

This is not really what I want because if I now search a new database, the program will list all games starting from 8...b5 and will include those with the very popular continuation 9 Bxf6. As I am only interested in encounters with 9 Nd5, I will be left with some superfluous games.

This is a case of ChessBase 8 being a bit too clever for its own good. The program wrongly 'guesses' that I am playing the Sveshnikov from Black's point of view and thus would be interested in all lines after 8...b5. Luckily, this problem can be corrected easily enough in a manual way. I first right-click on 8...b5, select **Special annotation** and **No critical position**. I then right-click on 9 Nd5, again select **Special annotation** and this time choose **Critical position-opening**. Now the program is ready to search for games from 9 Nd5. Using the search function on TWIC 426, it now lists both the Alekhine games and Sveshnikov games with 9 Nd5; there are nine overall. The more I add to my repertoire database, the more games there will be in this search result.

If you have many games/variations in your repertoire database, it is useful to use the function **Repertoire scan**, which is a quick and fancy way of finding out what's new in your opening systems. The program scans the new database in question and creates a report of all games which are in your repertoire. The report comes out as a database text and there are separate sections for each repertoire line. The games are given as links and can be clicked to be loaded. By selecting and merging all the games from one repertoire line, you can then choose the option **Print repertoire** to obtain a table-style summary (see page 105).

Chapter Three

Learning about Yourself... and your Opponents

In this chapter we shall be looking at the value of studying results at the chessboard and drawing conclusions, both from your own games and those of prospective opponents. Programs like ChessBase are powerful tools for generating statistics. The question is how can these be used in a positive way.

Mirror, Mirror on the Wall...

Every so often it makes sense to create a statistical survey of your results from all the different kinds of openings you play and the varying types of positions that you reach in your games. To provide an example, I'll again take my own results from the period 1996-2002. As this involves more than 500 games, it's a reasonable assumption to make that most of the statistics will provide a pretty accurate picture. On the other hand, for a serious player, I would recommend performing a statistical survey more than just once every seven years!

Using ChessBase, I create two opening books (or trees): one for my games with the white pieces (white9602.ctg) and one for my blacks (black9602.ctg). Using the search feature in ChessBase, I then collect all my white games (there are 274 of them) and drag and drop them into my tree of white games. Next I do a similar thing with my black games (there are only 264 of these – it looks like I've been a bit fortunate with colours).

Let's study the results of my white games first. In 274 games, my results were 139 wins, 108 draws and 26 losses (70 percent), against an average rating of 2417. The average rating performance during this time was 2532 and my rating performance in these games was 2567. So, as White, I performed on average 35 points over my rating.

In international chess, it's been worked out that, on average, White scores around 54 percent. Assuming similar ratings for those playing white and black, and using FIDE's rating performance chart, a score of 54 percent against a player of the same rating equates to around a 30-point jump in performance. Thus my performance here appears to be fairly normal and indicates neither excellence nor inferiority with the white pieces.

Now let's look at the results of the 273 games where I played 1 e4 (in the remaining game I ventured 1 Nf3). See Figure 14 for a breakdown of the results in ChessBase.

The top line of numbers shows my opponent's overall results against 1 e4, while beneath this there is a breakdown of results with all the different defences. Notice that the scores are shown from Black's point of view (ChessBase goes with whoever has the move). However, it is easy to calculate how well White is performing from these figures: if Black is, say, performing 30 points lower than his rating, then White must be performing 30 points higher than his. So, from the performance ratings in Figure 14, I can see that I've performed excellently against 1...d5, well against 1...c5, 1...e6, 1...g6 and 1...Nc6, reasonably against 1...c5 and 1...Nf6, poorly against 1...d6 and miserably against 1...c6. Taking my results against 1...c6 a little further, I click on 1...c6 and follow the branches. After 2 d4 d5 ChessBase shows me that I have a terrible record with the line 3 Nd2 dxe4 4 Nxe4 Nd7, and it's this that influences my overall score against the Caro-Kann. Disregarding the results of these games would make my score against the Caro-Kann much more convincing.

Delving deeper into this tree and performing a similar function with my games as Black, I quickly came to some more conclusions regarding my results in the 1996-2002 period:

1) I've performed well with the c3-Sicilian, but badly with 2 Nc3.

2) In open Sicilians, I've scored excellently against the Najdorf and the Dragon, but poorly against the Classical Variation (2 Nf3 d6 3 d4 cxd4 4 Nxd4 Nf6 5 Nc3 Nc6).

3) I've performed at 2600 with the French Tarrasch (1 e4 e6 2 d4 d5 3 Nd2).

4) My results are good in the main line Lopez, but not so convincing in offbeat lines.

5) As Black, my performance with the Sicilian has been much better than my performance with 1...e5.

6) Against 1 d4, I have an excellent score with the Nimzo-Indian, a reasonable score with the Queen's Indian, but a below-par score with the Modern Benoni.

7) My score against 1 c4 is not particularly good.

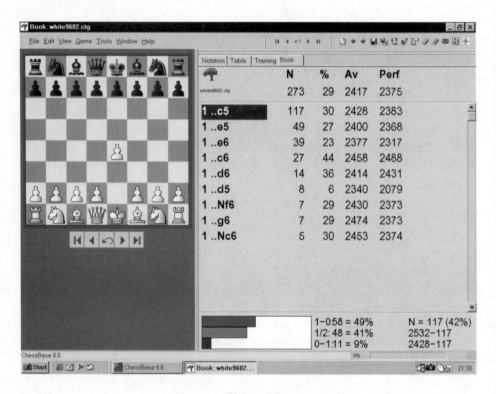

Figure 14

Statistics on different replies to 1 e4

There, I've revealed all my opening secrets now! However, I don't think I've let too much out of the bag, and anyone could have come to the same conclusions with the same ChessBase data at their disposal.

One thing that I should make absolutely clear is that it's very dangerous to come to any sweeping conclusions about how well you play certain openings and how well you know the theory simply on the statistics alone. The numbers are only there as a guideline and a prompt for further analysis. You should also bear in mind that factors like improvement – an improving player will naturally be performing higher than his published rating in any case.

If you really want to explore more deeply and reach correct assessments, you have to study the individual games and look how the results are related to the assessment of the position after the opening. For example, if you find that you are getting good results as White in the Open Sicilian despite getting lousy positions from the opening, this probably means that you have a natural flair for the positions, but would improve your score even more with some theoretical study. On the other hand, if you keep obtaining an edge out of the opening with the Ruy Lopez, but often fail to capitalise on this, then it's more likely that you do not understand the positions sufficiently and it may be time to try a new opening.

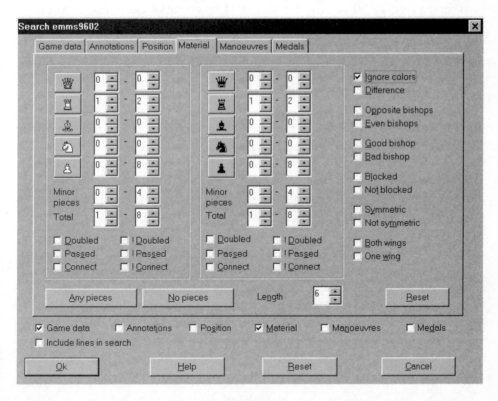

Figure 15

Searching for rook and pawn endings

When using statistics, you don't have to stick rigidly to openings. By using the 'position tab' in the search facility, you can search for games with different pawn structures (King's Indian, French, open Sicilian, Maroczy Bind, clear centre etc.).

Using the material tab, you can also look for different piece configurations.

In 1999 I wrote the book *The Survival Guide to Rook Endings*, a real eye-opener for me, after which I certainly believed I knew a lot more about rook endings than before. Still, I was curious to find out whether writing this book had any effect on my results in these endings. Using the search facility in Figure 15, I searched for my games that included rook and pawn endings both before and after I had written the book. Before the book, my average rating performance improved by 20 points in rook and pawn endings; after the book this figure increased to 60 points. Of course these figures don't prove anything, but I certainly feel more confident in rook and pawn endings these days. That said, in my last two rook and pawn endings I've failed to win despite being two pawns up on both occasions – there is certainly no room for complacency!

Preparing for Opponents

Let's assume that there is a reasonable amount of time to prepare against a specific opponent (this is not always the case), and that he (or she) has games in chess databases. Let's say that I am playing in an international tournament and due to play with the white pieces against the strong Hungarian Grandmaster Zoltan Almasi (I've played him a couple of times over the years). First I create a new database, calling it simply 'Almasi'. Then I look for his games in all the relevant databases (Mega Database, TWIC, Infobase etc.). To obtain these games I use ChessBase's players' index feature. As I've mentioned before, I have to take into account the various forms of his name. On this occasion there are only two, just 'Zoltan Almasi' and 'Z Almasi', but I must be careful not to include games from Istvan Almasi, who is his brother. Once I've located his games in a certain database, I simply drag and drop them into the 'Almasi' base.

After I've completed this stage with all the relevant databases, the next step is to eliminate the game doubles, as explained on page 29. Then I 'normalise' his name by editing it in the player's index of the new database, so that it was simply 'Zoltan Almasi'. In this particular case, this procedure is not strictly necessary because ChessBase's search feature would find 'Zoltan Almasi' if you entered 'Z Almasi' in the game data. However, you can see that normalising would be more important if you were dealing with Korchnoi, Kortschnoi, Kortchnoi etc.

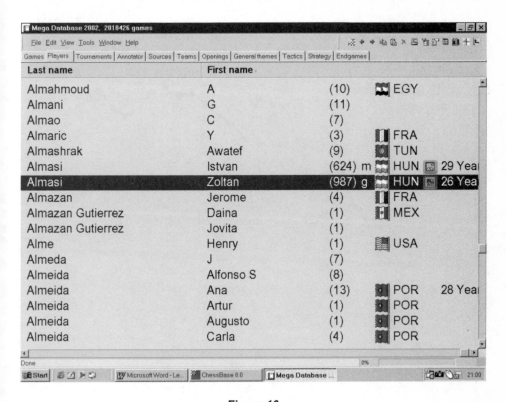

Figure 16

Finding Zoltan Almasi in the players' index

The final step before getting down to some analysis is to create two opening books (tree databases): one for his white games and one for his blacks. Even though I am playing white here, it can sometimes be useful to know what your opponent does with the white pieces, especially if he has any experience in your intended opening. Once I have created these books I can then begin to analyse both his games and his results with Black against my possible opening plans. Actually, one thing I've noticed about Almasi is that he has a much better score against 1 e4 than he does against 1 d4. Unfortunately, this information would be more useful to a player who is more flexible with the white pieces and plays 1 d4 as well as 1 e4 – I would have to challenge him on his own territory.

If I wanted even more information, I could go the whole hog and utilise the Players' Encyclopaedia, which includes a dossier on his openings, tournament results and lifetime results against individuals, a ratings profile (see Figure 17), and even photographs.

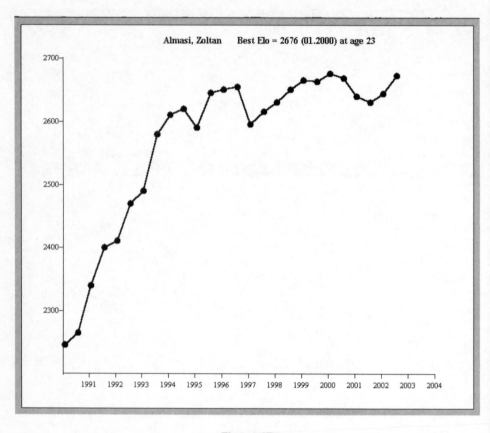

Figure 17

An Elo rating profile

Specific Preparation

Sometimes, if your opponent sticks rigidly to one opening system, it's possible to prepare very specifically the game. If you're thorough with your preparation (and perhaps a little fortunate), you can reach a position well into the game that you have already looked at in depth earlier on. Assuming that your opponent has been less thorough (you can't count on this!), this can become a big practical advantage for you, even if the resulting position is only objectively equal. You will have more 'experience' in the position and will be able to deal with plans and tactics more quickly, which is very important when the clock is ticking.

If you're very lucky, you might even be able to prepare the whole of the game! One occasion of this which springs to mind was when I was seconding Harriet Hunt at the World Girls Championship in 1997. In one of the later rounds, she was up against one of her main rivals, who tended to stick to the Caro-Kann Defence against 1 e4. With the help of fellow English player Richard Bates and, of course, Fritz, we were able to do some very useful preparation.

□ **H.Hunt** ■ **E.Danielian**

World Girls Championship, Zagan 1997

Caro-Kann Defence

1 e4 c6 2 d4 d5 3 exd5 cxd5 4 c4 Nf6 5 Nc3 e6 6 Nf3 Be7 7 cxd5 Nxd5 8 Bd3 0-0 9 0-0 Nc6 10 Re1 Bf6 11 Be4 Nce7 12 Ne5 g6

This line is known to be better for White, but we were fairly confident that Harriet would reach this position because Danielian tended to stick to the same variation and we already knew of two occasions where she had reached this position. However, we also spent a bit of time on the main move 12...Nc6 and a further alternative 12...Ng6, which Karpov had played a year earlier.

13 Bh6 Bg7 14 Qd2

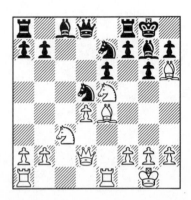

14...Nf6

According to ChessBase, Danielian's first experience with this line was a bit of a disaster: 14...b6 15 Ng4! Nf5 16 Bxf5 exf5 17 Bxg7 Kxg7 18 Qh6+ Kg8 19 Nxd5 fxg4 20 Ne7+ Kh8 21 Qf4 f6 22 Qh6 Bf5 23 Nc6 Qd5 24 Re7 Rf7 25 Rae1 Raf8 26 Re8 Qd6 27 R1e7 Qxe7 28 Rxe7 1-0 Grabics-Danielian, Hania 1994.

15 Rad1 Nxe4 16 Nxe4

16...Nf5

16...b6 17 Bxg7 Kxg7 18 Re3 Bb7 19 Rh3 h5 20 Ng3 Qd5 21 f3 Rh8 was unclear in the game Grabics-Danielian, Medellin 1996, which Black went on to win. It was this fact that led us to believe that she might well try the line again, and Harriet was ready with a big improvement in 18 Ng4!. In fact, Danielian deviated here with 16...Nf5, but our work still proved to be very beneficial, as the game soon transposes to our preparation.

17 Bxg7 Kxg7 18 Ng4! b6

19 Qc3!

The star move, although in the cold light of day it looks quite obvious. After 19 Qc3 Black is lost. White threatens d4-d5 and there is just no good way to protect all the weak dark squares around the king.

19...f6 20 Ngxf6! Rxf6 21 Nxf6 Kxf6

21...Qxf6 22 Qc6 wins the rook in the corner, as 22...Rb8 is met by 23 Qc7+.

22 d5+ e5

22...Kg5 23 dxe6 Qe7 24 Qd2+ Kf6 25 g4 Nh4 26 Qd5 wins for White.

23 Qc6+ 1-0

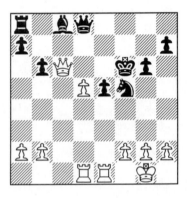

White wins the rook on a8. This is the exactly the position we had in front of us the morning before the game! Harriet played brilliantly to win the tournament and fought in some extremely tough battles, but this wasn't one of them.

I can't, off the top of my head, think of any occasions when this has happened in one of my games, but there have been occasions when I have reached a position well into the game which I had previously studied at home. The following game, against fellow English GM Keith Arkell was very pleasing in this respect.

□ **Arkell** ■ **Emms**

Hastings 1995/96

Modern Benoni

---

1 d4 Nf6 2 Nf3 e6 3 c4 c5 4 d5 d6 5 Nc3 exd5 6 cxd5 g6 7 g3 Bg7 8 Bg2 0-0 9 0-0 Re8 10 Nd2 a6 11 a4 Nbd7 12 Nc4

Characteristically, Keith chooses the solid approach. The main line runs 12 h3 Rb8 and only now 13 Nc4. After 13...Ne5 14 Na3 play can become very tactical.

12...Ne5 13 Nxe5 Rxe5 14 Qc2

Keith has also played 14 Bf4 here, for example 14...Re8 15 Qc2 Nh5 16 Bd2 f5 17 Rab1 f4! 18 gxf4 Qh4 19 e3 Bf5 20 Ne4 g5! 21 Nf6+! Nxf6 22 Qxf5 gxf4 23 Qxf4 Qxf4 24 exf4 Re2 with good compensation for the pawn, Arkell-Emms, British League 1997.

14...Rh5!?

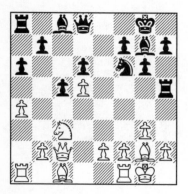

This slightly optimistic move was one that I analysed with Chris Ward, who also plays the Modern Benoni with Black and has had a couple of battles with Keith. The idea is very provocative as it allows White to move pawns forward with tempo. However, we had a very specific plan in mind. I was just lucky enough to be the first one who had the chance to play it.

15 e4

White logically advances in the centre to try and take advantage of Black's 'offside' rook. Using ChessBase, the only game I had seen before this had continued 15 h4 Re5 (the rook has done its job on h5 now that White has weakened the g4-square) 16 Rb1 Re8 17 b4 cxb4 18 Rxb4 Bg4 with a roughly level position in Khalifman-Shabalov USSR 1986.

15...Ng4!? 16 h3 Nf6 17 g4 Bxg4

The only logical way to continue.

18 hxg4 Nxg4 19 Bf4 Qh4

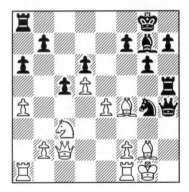

20 Bg3

After some thought, Keith decided to opt for an endgame. As well as this move, Chris and I had studied both 20 Bxd6 and 20 Rfd1, both of which lead to very unclear complications.

20...Qxg3! 21 fxg3 Bd4+ 22 Rf2 Bxf2+ 23 Qxf2 Nxf2 24 Kxf2

This is the position which I had looked at before the game. In my opinion Black is slightly better and I was eventually able to convert my successful preparation into a win.

A Little Knowledge is a Dangerous Thing

If only I could boast of hundreds of spectacular ChessBase and Fritz-inspired opening novelties. Alas, for every story of good, thorough preparation, there is the opposite – a bad, rushed concoction of an opening idea. I'm sure that most people reading this have had occasions where it's five minutes before the game and you still don't know what to play! Even with tools such as ChessBase and Fritz, it's difficult when you reach this situation.

Sometimes a little knowledge is a dangerous thing when it comes to openings. Before this game, I had found some neat trick for Black on ChessBase. Unfortunately, my preparation was so rushed and disorganised that by the time I reached the board, I was rather confused.

☐ **Lalic** ■ **Emms**

Southend 2001

Queen's Indian Defence

1 d4 Nf6 2 c4 e6 3 Nf3 b6 4 g3 Ba6 5 Qa4 Bb7 6 Bg2 c5 7 dxc5

bxc5 8 0-0 Be7 9 Nc3 0-0

This was the first time I had played this line of the Queen's Indian Defence. I had studied it a little, but had no practice in offhand games and it soon became clear that my little knowledge would actually hinder me.

10 Bf4 Qb6 11 Rad1

During the game I was trying to remember a line which contains a venomous trap. Actually, the variation is 11 Rfd1 d6 12 Rd2 Nc6! 13 Bxd6 Bxd6 14 Rxd6 Qxb2 15 Rb1 Qxc3 16 Rxb7 Nd4!

and Black has a fully acceptable position. The sting in the tail here is that the seemingly natural 17 Nxd4?? actually loses at once to 17...Qe1+ 18 Bf1 Ne4!, which has happened in both Dautov-Palac, Vienna 1996 and Istratescu-N.Pedersen, Kavala 2002 – two strong Grandmasters falling for the same trick.

Now I know that Bogdan's move order is more accurate as it avoids the trick – the move ...Qxb2 no longer attacks a rook on a1. However, during the excitement of the game I became confused and began to look for a trap that simply wasn't there.

11...d6 12 Rd2 Rd8

12...Nc6 13 Bxd6 Bxd6 14 Rxd6 Qxb2 is still playable for Black but is less effective when there is no hanging rook on a1.

13 Rfd1 Nc6?

Somehow I knew that this move was wrong and I had even foreseen Bogdan's 16th move. It was just that I couldn't get this 'trick' out of my mind and just couldn't resist playing ...Nc6. Simply 13...h6 or

13...Ne8 is stronger.

14 Bxd6 Bxd6 15 Rxd6 Qxb2

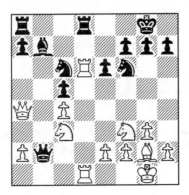

16 Qb5!

My warped thinking had led me to a highly unlikely line that contains a similar trap – 16 Rxd8+ Rxd8 17 Rb1? Qxc3 18 Rxb7 Nd4! 19 Nxd4? Qe1+ 20 Bf1 Ng4 and Black wins. However, after White's actual choice Black can do nothing but enter a miserable ending in which his weak queenside pawns give White a clear plus.

16...Qxb5 17 cxb5 Rxd6 18 Rxd6 Nb4 19 Ne5 Bxg2 20 Kxg2 Kf8 21 e4! Ke7 22 Rd2

Threatening a2-a3. Black must give up a pawn.

22...c4 23 Rd4

and White eventually converted his extra pawn.

So, as highlighted in Chapter 2, before embarking on a competitive game, it really pays to familiarise yourself with an opening by first playing it in offhand games against a training partner, on the net, or against a chess engine. This would certainly minimise the number of accidents like the one above.

Chapter Four

Relating Openings to Middlegames and Endgames

Analysing an Opening Backwards

I am not completely sure who it was gave me the idea to study openings backwards – once upon a time long ago, when laptops and databases were just starting to become a standard tool for young hopeful players such as me. I think it was grandmaster Tiger Hillarp-Persson from Sweden, but I am far from certain. I somehow remember English super-grandmaster Matthew Sadler's name mentioned somewhere in that connection, but it is possible I am mistaken about this. But this has little importance, as the method described below has grown from nothing more than vaguely described principles which have come my way. So any shortcomings in the method are to be blamed on me and not the grandmasters.

Personally, I have used the method of backward analysis mainly for writing introductions to my opening books *The Panov-Botvinnik Attack* and *The Dutch Stonewall.* But I would really have liked to use it more on my own opening repertoire, as it is the best way I know to improve your general opening knowledge – and thereby your over-the-board results. It seems it is not only me who is interested in this method as, when I mentioned the idea *en passant* in my book *Excelling at Chess*, I got quite a lot of questions asking how it was actually done.

In his acclaimed book *Secrets of Practical Chess* Dr. John Nunn recommends that you should play through a number of complete games when you start to study a new opening. This is of course very beneficial, and probably the way most people try to learn the strategy behind an opening system. But for me personally this alone is not satisfying. First of all I tend to forget games I play through. Secondly, I always seem to study the wrong games or read the wrong annotations. One example concerned opposite-coloured bishops in the Sveshnikov variation of the Sicilian. I had read that in positions such as the one below, the exchange of bishop for knight favoured Black, if he could get his bishop to e5. I later learned that this is absolutely not the case at all.

□ Kreuzholz ■ Aagaard

Germany 1999

Sicilian Defence

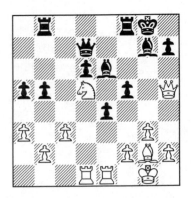

In this position I reacted according to the knowledge I thought I possessed and went for a position with opposite-coloured bishops, believing that it would be fine for me, though probably drawish in nature. Unfortunately the guidelines I was following, as described in the annotations to a game by a Grandmaster, were far from exact, and my position soon was far from being either fine or drawish. It must be said that I then made matters worse by dropping a pawn in calculation. The game finished:

22...b4? 23 axb4 Bxd5 24 Rxd5 axb4 25 Bh3 Be5? 26 Rxe4 bxc3 27 bxc3 Qb7 28 Rh4 Rf6 29 c4 Rbf8 30 Bg2 Qa7 31 Ra5 Qc7 32 Bd5+ Kh8 33 Rb5 h6 34 Rb7 Qc5 35 Qxh6+ 1-0

Later I made a simple search in my database and discovered that White generally won these kinds of positions – which is actually logical, as the white bishop dominates the light squares, which automatically makes all the black pawns on the kingside weak. The search in ChessBase was a basic exploitation of the **Material** function in the **Search Mask**, as well as setting the **Game Data** for ECO: B33-B33 (the Encyclopaedia Code for the Sveshnikov variation) and Elo at a minimum of 2200 for both players. The **Material Search** looked something like this (see Figure 18).

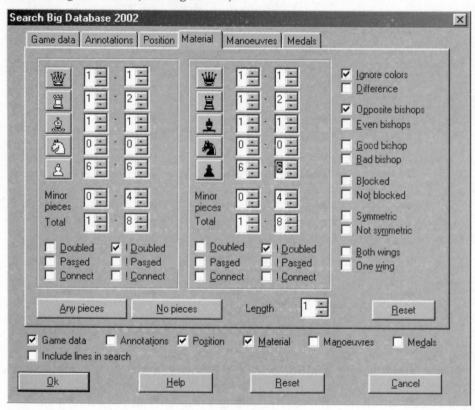

Figure 18

Using a material search

The positions I was looking for were middlegames, therefore with one queen each and a minimum of one rook. Knights were no longer a part of the game and both players were restricted to one bishop, which were supposed to be of opposite colours. Finally I chose six pawns each, as I had had in my game, as this is the standard situation. And of course, none of these pawns were allowed to be doubled.

My search results this time around gave me 61 games with these properties. For me that is more or less perfect. I can quickly play through most of them, as I am looking for whatever makes these games different from each other. The following positions give a good indication of when the exchange is justified, based on comparison.

☐ **Karpov** ■ **Nunn**

Phillips & Drew, London 1982
Sicilian Defence

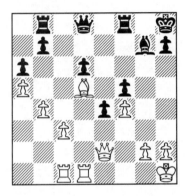

White won.

☐ **Luther** ■ **Krasenkov**

Bundesliga 1998/99
Sicilian Defence

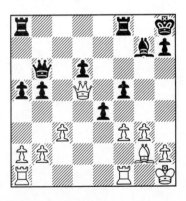

After **23...e3 24 f4 b4** Black won.

□ **Voitsekhovsky** ■ **Grebionkin**

Novgorod 1998

Sicilian Defence

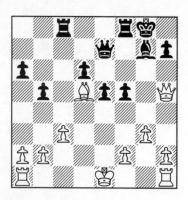

White won.

□ **Kovacevic** ■ **Kramnik**

Leningrad 1991

Sicilian Defence

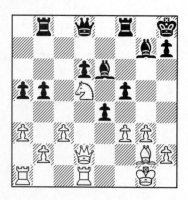

Black won well after:

22...Bxd5 23 Qxd5 Be5!

Played with the idea of 24 fxe4 f4! and the dark squares around the white king become mortally weak.

24 Rd2 exf3 25 Bxf3 Qg5 26 Re1 Qf6 27 Ree2 Rg8 28 Kf1 Rg5 29

Qc6 Rf8

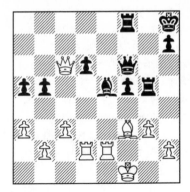

30 Qb6 h5 31 Rf2 Qg6 32 Be4 h4 33 gxh4 Rg1+ 34 Ke2 Qg4+ 35 Bf3 Qc4+ 36 Rd3 Bxc3 37 bxc3 Re8+ 0-1

My conclusion at the time, which I hold to this day, is that Black needs to have active counterplay available in order to be able to go into positions with opposite-coloured bishops. In the Krasenkow game Black had the passed pawn, allowing White no peace of mind to organise an attack on the light squares. In the Kramnik example Black sacrificed a pawn to make sure he took over the initiative. In the Karpov and Voitsekhovsky examples Black did not have these kind of resources and neither did I in my own game.

A comparison between the two methods seems to give pluses and minuses to both. The old method is probably a little more relaxed, more enjoyable and takes less time. The only problem with it is that it is not very reliable. The method that I will describe below is more accurate, but has the disadvantage of being more time consuming. But the advantage is that this method can either be used systematically as described below, or be used to get answers to specific questions as described above.

There is also another great plus for the analytical method compared with the 'going over some games' method. There is nothing so unreliable as your feeling for statistics. A concrete analysis of a specific theme in any position will always give you a more reliable base.

The Principle of the Method of Backward Analysis

The main idea of analysing an opening backwards is that you then know what you are aiming for, which is a most valuable tool when you are trying to solve middlegame or even opening problems at the board. Most strong players have a general idea about what is right and what is wrong, but this is far from flawless, and many endgames have been entered with a wrong evaluation and/or been misplayed by players who should know better. The main principle is that: *You can never know enough about any specific type of position.* Most of the examples you see in opening books are clear-cut, simply because the writer wants to avoid ambiguity. But real life, in this case over-the-board play, is filled with ambiguity. In my own 1999 book on the Sveshnikov variation I used the game Voitsekhovsky-Grebionkin as an illustration of the dangers in the position. But as we can see above, matters are more complex and the evaluation of a position can quickly change once the properties of the position do so.

It was practically impossible for me to include a deeper discussion of this element of positional evaluation in a book concentrated on theoretical analysis of a fashionable opening, but in my opinion it is no less relevant to the player looking to improve his practical results. Knowing the endgames of your openings well gives you a lot of freedom in the middlegame, where you do not have to evaluate the consequences of different exchanges exhaustively, as the main properties of the resulting endgames will already be known to you.

As for the following investigation of typical middlegame motifs, then the advantages of this method are many. First of all you will not have to sit and ponder on where you should put the pieces or which is the better of two possible plans. Secondly you will find the transition from opening to middlegame less problematic. I remember some talented Danish juniors who used all their energy on studying concrete theoretical lines. Often they would play the first 20 moves of the opening very quickly knowing everything very well, but once these moves had passed they didn't know how to continue and too often lost level or adventurous positions in a very few moves. Knowing what you should do with your position is in my opinion just as important as memorising theoretical lines. Although this does depend on which opening we are discussing. In very sharp positions it is often necessary to know exactly what you are doing, or there is a real chance that you will lose the game more or less before it has begun. For instance, if you play the open Sicilian as White, it is necessary to do some home preparation on positions such as the following, also taken from the Sveshnikov variation. This time it is a highly tactical line where White sacrifices a bishop for two pawns and some threats.

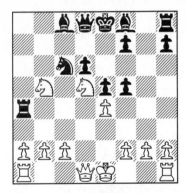

To me it is obvious that knowledge of different endgames plays little importance in this position, as most endgames reached from here will be decided in advance or be highly irregular. But these lines are reached in a limited number of games. These days most white players find memorising variations and keeping up to date with theory tiring, and if you do play the Sveshnikov as Black, it is my guess that you have just as much chance of ending up in the following position (after 1 e4 c5 2 Nf3 Nc6 3 Bb5 e6 4 0-0 Nge7 5 Re1 a6 6 Bf1):

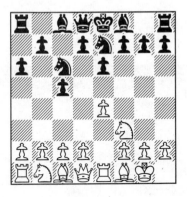

Now we are suddenly talking strategy as much as tactics and here a full analysis of the games in your database is helpful.

How is this kind of analysis performed?

In the example above with the opposite-coloured bishops I had an easy task, as I already knew a lot about the position I wanted to understand. To analyse an opening backwards naturally takes more work. Instead of presenting some abstract idea of how to do it, I will take your through an analysis of the French Tarrasch with 3...Nf6, i.e. the lines after 1 e4 e6 2 d4 d5 3 Nd2 Nf6. Here my own choice would be the line 4 e5 Nfd7 5 Bd3 (instead of the more reckless 5 f4) 5...c5 6 c3, when Black has a choice of 6...b6 and the absolute main line 6...Nc6 7 Ne2 and so on. It is all in the theory books. That is, except for the analysis I now want to perform.

The French Tarrasch, C05-C06

The first thing I do, when I have narrowed down the subject to a particular line, is to create a new database for the games I am interested in, and copy into it all the relevant games from my main database. Opening the Big Database 2002, which I happen to be using, in there I click on Openings and find my way through the *ECO* codes. Now I know that I am looking for C05-C06, but if I didn't then I would be able to find the relevant codes by simply looking for the moves.

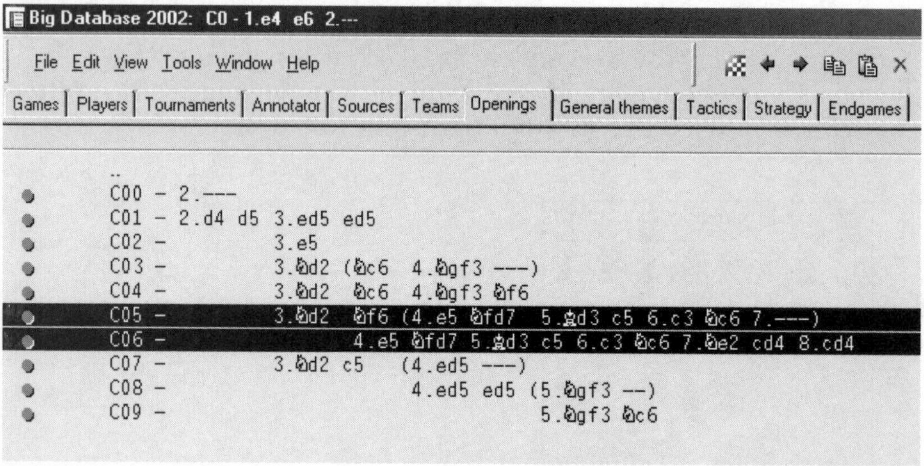

Figure 19

Isolating the relevant ECO codes

After highlighting the relevant codes I copy all games to the clipboard and then drag and drop them into my new database C05-C06. By creating this new database I gain several advantages. First of all I can delete any games that are of little interest for me and disregard them once and for all. Secondly, my subsequent search time will be limited to less than a second, whereas it is about 2 minutes when searching for positions in the Big Database.

In my C05-C06 database I now have 14,876 games played in the

French Tarrasch with 3...Nf6. But obviously there will be some that are of little use to me in my study of the endgame. So I search in turn for games with the following properties:

- Games finished before move 30. I am analysing endgames. I will create a new database for middlegames later.

- Games by players with less than 2200 average Elo played after 1985. Unrated games before 1985 are normally games between quite strong players, whereas after this time it became custom to store all games played in tournaments, and unrated games after 1985 are normally played between unrated players and not Grandmasters.

- Games with the white pawn on f4 before move 10, as this never occurs in the line I want to investigate.

After finding these games I delete them, which I do this by first highlighting them all and then pressing delete.

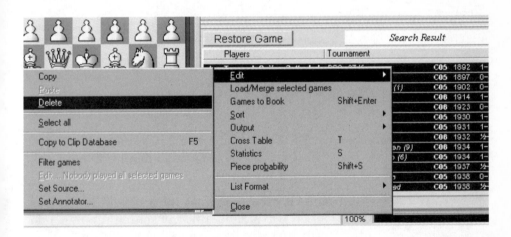

Figure 20

Deleting irrelevant games

However, this does not immediately remove the games from the database in the program I use, so I need to do this with another command: **Remove Deleted Games** in ChessBase 8 and **Physical Deletions** under the **Technical**-menu in ChessBase 7. I have to remember to remove deleted games after each of my searches, as otherwise I would risk double-deleting some games, which is the same as cancelling the deletion. And that of course is not what I want.

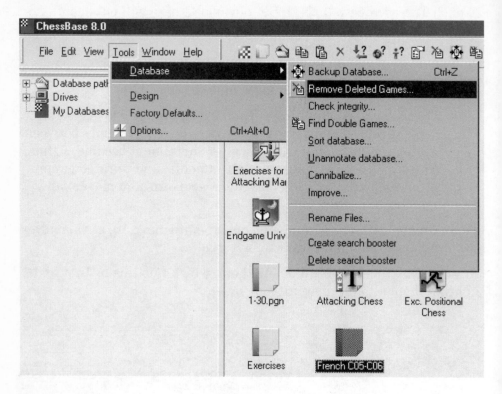

Figure 21

Removing unwanted games

I have now reduced my C05-C06 database to 3,956 games. Of course I cannot get anything coherent from scanning this amount of games, so I now turn to the second part of my work.

With the database limited to all the relevant endgames of this rather big line, I now start to look at ways to narrow my search further. I do this by moving all the games to the clipboard and then organise them according to rating (see Figure 22).

Having done this I now play the games through from the beginning in order to find the relevant pawn structures and piece configurations. This is done in order to narrow down the search even further. To make sure I do not overlook anything, I simply write down all the relevant structures on a piece of paper. I play through about 100 games, or until no new structures worth taking notice of appear in the games. This way I quickly get a list worth working with.

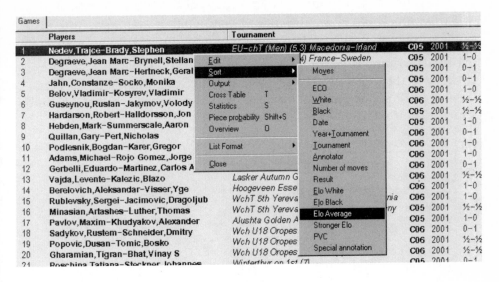

	Players	Tournament				
1	Nedev,Trajce–Brady,Stephen	EU–chT (Men) (5.3) Macedonia–Irland		C05	2001	½–½
2	Degraeve,Jean Marc–Brynell,Stellan		4) France–Sweden	C05	2001	1–0
3	Degraeve,Jean Marc–Hertneck,Geral			C05	2001	0–1
4	Jahn,Constanze–Socko,Monika		Moves	C05	2001	0–1
5	Belov,Vladimir–Kosyrev,Vladimir		ECO	C06	2001	1–0
6	Guseynou,Ruslan–Jakymov,Volody		White	C06	2001	½–½
7	Hardarson,Robert–Halldorsson,Jon		Black	C05	2001	½–½
8	Hebden,Mark–Summerscale,Aaron		Date	C05	2001	1–0
9	Quillan,Gary–Pert,Nicholas		Year+Tournament	C06	2001	0–1
10	Podlesnik,Bogdan–Karer,Gregor		Tournament	C06	2001	1–0
11	Adams,Michael–Rojo Gomez,Jorge		Annotator	C06	2001	1–0
12	Gerbelli,Eduardo–Martinez,Carlos A		Number of moves	C06	2001	0–1
13	Vajda,Levente–Kalezic,Blazo	Lasker Autumn G	Result	C06	2001	½–½
14	Berelovich,Aleksandar–Visser,Yge	Hoogeveen Esse	Elo White	C06	2001	1–0
15	Rublevsky,Sergei–Jacimovic,Dragoljub	WchT 5th Yereva	Elo Black	C06	2001	½–½
16	Minasian,Artashes–Luther,Thomas	WchT 5th Yereva	Elo Average	C05	2001	1–0
17	Pavlov,Maxim–Khudyakov,Alexander	Alushta Golden A	Stronger Elo	C05	2001	1–0
18	Sadykov,Rustem–Schneider,Dmitry	Wch U18 Oropes	PVC	C06	2001	0–1
19	Popovic,Dusan–Tomic,Bosko	Wch U18 Oropes	Special annotation	C06	2001	½–½
20	Gharamian,Tigran–Bhat,Vinay S	Wch U18 Oropes		C06	2001	½–½
21	Roschina,Tatiana–Steckner,Johannes	Winterthur on 1st (7)		C05	2001	0–1

Menu items shown: Edit, Sort, Output, Cross Table (T), Statistics (S), Piece probability (Shift+S), Overview (O), List Format, Close

Figure 22

Sorting games by ELO-rating

On the way I might find specific positions, which are not general, but might still be good to remember. I save these into a new database I have created and save my conclusions for later. The first endgame of this type is the following:

□ **Rublevsky** ■ **Ulibin**
St. Petersburg 1998

The game was soon drawn. As I said earlier, most Grandmasters would use very little time to make sure that this position is a draw, but you also have to find it first. Still, it is not the knowledge of one or

two positions that will make a significant difference in practical play, but the knowledge of a multitude of positions.

After having gone through some games I find nine different pawn structures that I want to investigate further. I do this in a similar fashion to the one I used to investigate the Sveshnikov above. This time it is all about pawn structures. The first structure that I decide to investigate is the following:

The way to do this is not to search for this specific structure, as there are a lot of similar positions that I would then exclude from my search. Let us say that the h-pawn is on h3 instead of h2. This makes little difference to my investigation of the structure. The same goes for the b-pawn, which might often be on b3 instead of b2.

Therefore I search in the following way: I use the 'Exclude' board function as illustrated below, and Material search in which I ask for 5-5 pawns and 0-0 queens for a length of 10 moves. This will ensure that I get the right kind of endgames, and endgames in which it was actually worth playing on (see Figure 23)

This search leaves me with 70 games. I transfer these to the clipboard and finally I have something worth working with.

I can now ask for general statistics – these give White a 64% score, well over the average (which is 55%). But the main thing is that I have reduced the number of games to an amount I can handle. I now sort the games according to the number of moves, because normally, the longer the games are, the more they reflect the correct evaluation of the endgame (though I can know nothing for sure before I run through the games of course).

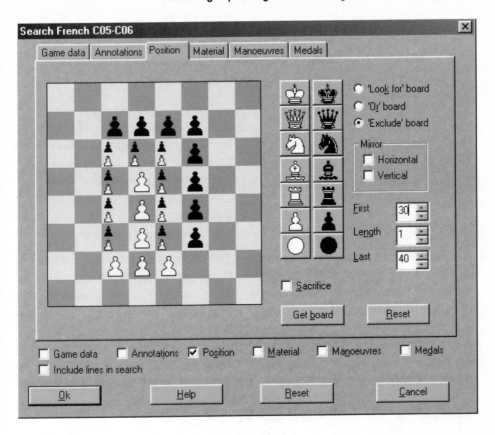

Figure 23

Searching for endgames without pawns on certain squares

Still, my most important analysis of the position comes from simply organising the games according to ELO average and playing them through from the top. As with everything in the magical world of computers there comes a time when you have to think for yourself. The computer is a brilliant and willing slave, but I can assure you that it is also a cruel and deceptive master. You have to look through the games yourself and draw your own conclusions. I strongly recommend against using Fritz to evaluate these kinds of positions. Fritz will not give a correct evaluation of any of these endgames. Recently an 11-year old pupil of mine told me that the Sicilian Dragon was bad for Black, because Fritz liked the white positions better! The Sicilian Dragon might very well be dubious for all I care, but I would play it against Fritz with pleasure if I had the advantage of referring to opening books, and Fritz had to think for itself.

The only reliable hint that you can get in your evaluation is the results of the games between Grandmasters. Often when one side loses, he might have been able to draw with better play. The fact that he does not find the moves gives us an indication that it is *difficult* to find them. And in practical play this means a disadvantage.

The way I want to analyse the 70 games I have collected is to run through them and see if I can spot any patterns emerging. Here it can be a good idea first to sort the games by **Result** in order to see under what circumstances the games are won for White, when they are drawn and lost. But what I personally always trust most are Elo ratings. Strong players also mishandle good endgames and blunder pieces away, but they do it less frequently. So, generally, these games are more reliable for the evaluation of the different positions.

My search this time ended up with a few different positions, which I save into my **French Endgames** database, in which I also saved the Rublevsky game above. When I save the games I normally remove the beginning moves of the game, as this database is for general endgame knowledge, not for memorising theory. If I wanted to be really efficient I could remove the moves completely from some of the games and only keep single positions with evaluations. Normally I would not do this, but it is a matter of taste I suppose. I have only done so below to save space. The comments that replace the moves are the same as I would add to the database alongside the moves.

□ **Rausis** ■ **Farago**
Germany 1996
French Defence

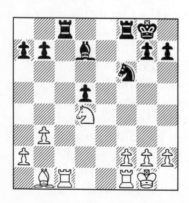

This seems to be a prototypically good endgame for White. In the minor piece ending Black has problems getting his pieces to play properly, while White makes a fluent invasion in the centre as he advances his pawns on the kingside. The knight is well placed on d4.

21 f3 b6 22 Bd3 a5 23 a3 Rxc1 24 Rxc1 Rc8 25 Rxc8+ Bxc8 26 Kf2 Kf7 27 Ke3 Ke7 28 h4 Kd6 29 g4 h6 30 Bf5 Ba6 31 f4 Ng8 32 h5 Nf6 33 Kf3 Bb7 34 Bg6 Ke7 35 g5 Ne4 36 Bxe4 dxe4+ 37 Ke3

37...Bd5 38 b4 axb4 39 axb4 Bf7 40 Nf5+ Kf8 41 Ng3 Bb3 42 Kxe4 Kf7 43 Ke5 hxg5 44 fxg5 Bc2 45 g6+ Kf8 46 Kf4 Bb1 47 Kg5 Bd3 48 Nf5 Kg8 49 Nd4 Bc4 50 Kf5 Bf1 51 Kg5 Bc4 52 h6 gxh6+ 53 Kxh6 Ba2 54 Kg5 Kf8 55 Kf6 Ke8 56 g7 Bg8 57 Nf5 Bh7 58 Nh6 Kd7 59 Ke5 1-0

□ **Vokarev** ■ **Volkov**

Russia 2000

French Defence

Black managed to make a draw here because his pieces were active, but it still looked uncomfortable for him. (In this position White played 28 Rb3.)

☐ **Lyrberg** ■ **Moskalenko**
Helsinki 1992
French Defence

This position appears to be completely drawn no matter what anybody does. It makes little difference if the d-pawn is on d5 or d4, something I learned from the next position. This game was drawn after:

30 Ke3 Ke5 31 Bc2 Rf4 32 Rc1 Rf6 33 Rd1 Rf4 34 Rc1 Rf6 35 Rd1 Re6 36 Bd3 Bd7 37 Rc1 Rb6 38 b4 Rc6 39 Re1 Rf6 40 g3 Bc6 41 Be2 Re6 42 Rd1 Kd6+ 43 Kf2 Re8 44 Rd4 Ke5 45 Ke3

45...Bb5 46 Bxb5 axb5 47 h4 Ra8 48 hxg5 hxg5 49 f4+ gxf4+ 50 gxf4+ Kd6 51 Rd3 Re8+ 52 Kf3 Re1 53 Rc3 ½-½

□ Larsen ■ Agdestein

Finland 1989

French Defence

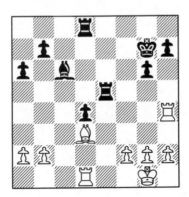

The game was drawn without much of a fight.

□ Kindermann ■ Bunzmann

Germany 1998

French Defence

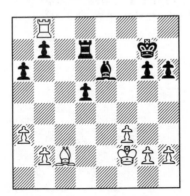

The strong position of the white rook in this game was enough to ensure White of the victory. Still I must not forget that White has 200 Elo points more than his opponent.

36...Kf6 37 Ke3 d4+ 38 Ke2 Bc4+ 39 Bd3 Bd5 40 Rh8 Kg7 41 Rc8 Rd6 42 Bc4 Bc6 43 Rc7+ Kf8 44 h4 b5 45 Ba2 Bd7 46 Rc5 Ke7 47 Bb1 Bc6 48 Be4 Bd7 49 g4 Be8 50 b4 a5 51 Kd3 axb4 52 axb4 Bd7 53 g5 hxg5 54 hxg5 Bh3 55 Re5+ Kf7 56 Bd5+ Kf8 57 Kxd4

Bf1 58 Re6 Rd8 59 Rxg6 1-0

☐ **Zapata** ■ **Chernin**
Subotica 1987
French Defence

This must be a complete dream position for White with good knight against bad bishop. Nevertheless, the a3-pawn gives him a few technical problems.

42...R3e7 43 h4 Ra8 44 Ra2 Ra5 45 Rd4 Be8 46 Nb4 Bf7 47 Nc2 Kf6 48 Rb4 Be8 49 Ne3 Ke5 50 Rd2 Bc6 51 Nc2 Kd6 52 Rbd4 Ra8 53 R2d3 Kc5

54 Ne3 Kb6 55 b4 Rae8 56 Nxd5+ Bxd5 57 Rxd5 Re2+ 58 Kg3 Ra2 59 Rg5 Ree2 60 Kh3 Ra1 61 Rd7 1-0

These were the endgames I found it important to remember after going through the games. I am not really interested in pure rook endings, or knight vs. bishop, as I have good appreciation of the first through general endgame knowledge, and the second seems so obviously good for White. The Rausis game is one example. However, I was not so sure how to assess the pure knight endings. So I searched the clipboard for pure knight endings using the material search criteria **No pieces** and then 1-1 on knights, which gave me five games. And I think no matter how lazy you are, you can always play through five games. The one which I found relevant was the following:

☐ **Psakhis** ■ **Riazantsev**

Ubeda 2001

French Defence

This seems like a draw, but it is all about the position of the kings I guess.

33...Ne5 34 f4 Nd3 35 b3 g6 36 g5 Nc1 37 a3 Nd3 38 b4 a5 39 bxa5
½-½

I will stop here and omit the other eight pawn structures I found important enough to investigate. The main mission has been to show what I would do with the analytical method, not to analyse the French Tarrasch.

It is obvious that I could have performed this analysis differently. I made some choices on the way that can be discussed. First of all I did not examine things very deeply, but only took a few basic positions and made some basic assessments. This is very useful for repetition later. I just open my French Endgames folder and play through the examples. I already have written down my conclusions, so I do not have to start again investigating the positions even if I have completely forgotten them, which I probably will have.

Another great advantage with having more or less prototypical endgames available are their value as training material. You can take the positions from your file and play them against Fritz, or even better, against a friend. The main problem with playing these positions against Fritz is that it is hard not to try to beat it. As Fritz has some enormous strengths in complications you might develop a tendency to avoid complications even when they are good for you. But if you, like me, have strong self-confidence and very little respect for this bunch of chips (give me some ketchup please!), it is not really a problem.

Here you see me lose a 3 minute game against Fritz in an attempt to prove an advantage:

□ Aagaard ■ Fritz 7
Blitz Game, Copenhagen 2003
French Defence

---

1 e4 e6 2 d4 d5 3 Nd2 Nf6 4 e5 Nfd7 5 c3 c5 6 Bd3 Nc6 7 Ne2 Qb6 8 Nf3 cxd4 9 cxd4 f6 10 exf6 Nxf6 11 0-0 Bd6 12 b3 0-0 13 Bf4 Bxf4 14 Nxf4 Bd7 15 Rc1 Rae8 16 Bb1 Nxd4 17 Qxd4 Qxd4 18 Nxd4 e5 19 Nfe2 exd4 20 Nxd4 Rc8

Here Fritz started on an adventure of its own. I got a good position and then tried for tactics with 30 h4!?. Probably 33 f4 was just a mistake after which I was struggling. Then the endgame became tactical and Fritz showed me no mercy.

21 f3 Kf7 22 Kf2 b5 23 Bd3 a6

Humans would not normally get away with putting all their pawns on the same colour as the bishop in the endgame, but for some strange reason I refrained from the thematic 24 b4!, fearing that c4 would be too weak. Instead I played 24 g4 after which Black soon had most of his pawns on the dark squares and I had pawns on the light squares. This tells something about me not paying enough attention to this and therefore being punished.

24 g4 g5 25 h3 b4 26 Ke3 Rfe8+ 27 Kd2 h5 28 Rxc8 Rxc8 29 a4 a5 30 h4!? gxh4 31 g5 Ne8 32 Rh1 h3

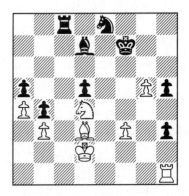

33 f4? Nd6 34 f5 Rg8 35 g6+ Kf6 36 Rxh3 Rxg6 37 Rxh5 Rg2+ 38 Ke3 Rg3+ 39 Ke2

39...Ne4 40 Rh6+ Ke5 41 Nf3+ Kxf5 42 Rd6 Kf4 43 Rxd7 Nc3+ 44 Ke1 Kxf3 45 Re7 Rg2 46 Ra7 Ke3 47 Bf1 Rb2 48 Re7+ Ne4 49 Kd1 Rb1+ 50 Kc2 Rxf1 0-1

Middlegame Analysis

I have explained why it is a good idea to start off analysing the end-game, but of course when we play we usually have to pass through the middlegame first. And though many players suffer from a dislike of the endgame, the middlegame is the place where we truly meet our mediocrity. Opening theory can be memorised and studied to eternity. In fact, today we do not even have to think for ourselves in the open-ing, we can turn on Fritz at home and BOOM, we come up with an improvement to our pet line, or maybe just an interesting new move. But the middlegame, well that is a challenge for the ages.

Luckily we can prepare ourselves considerably for the middlegames in our repertoire without too much trouble. It will of course never be anything more than a supplement to independent thinking, but any-thing that can help us in our troubles is good. But imagine this: not having to struggle evaluating very complex positional aspects, nor having to struggle to find a plan, but in most situations merely calcu-lating how to implement one of the different ideas you already know.

There was a series by Batsford in the 90's which tried to do this kind of analysis. It was called the *Mastering the...* (insert an opening) – in this example *Mastering the French* (McDonald & Harley), or Spanish, King's Indian or Benoni. I really like these books because of what they do, though I also see their limitations. Due to lack of space they can only talk abstractly about middlegame concepts. After this there are a couple of illustrative games, which have usually been picked not be-cause they are typical, but exciting. It is a good place to start analysis, but not really very useful in itself.

What I would do is not very different from the way I treated the end-game. I would simply go into my **French C05-C06** file and sort the games according to Elo average. Then play through the games from the top and look for concepts in the middlegame.

Before moving on I think I should explain what a middlegame concept is. A middlegame concept is a recurring theme, or a theme you believe can be recurring at least. It is a typical manoeuvre, an exchange, a positional sacrifice or a combination. Below you will see plenty of ex-amples.

When I notice a middlegame concept, I write it down on a piece of pa-per and then continue. It is not my intention to evaluate it in any way or form. That will come later. I normally get a good sense for which

concepts are important, so when at some point I feel that no significant new concepts are appearing in the games, I stop and go to the
second part of my middlegame analysis – the narrow database search.

Let us say that the first concept that interests me is a white bishop on
b5 capturing a knight on c6 in order to gain control over e5. I then
make a search based on **Manoeuvres** as in the Figure 24:

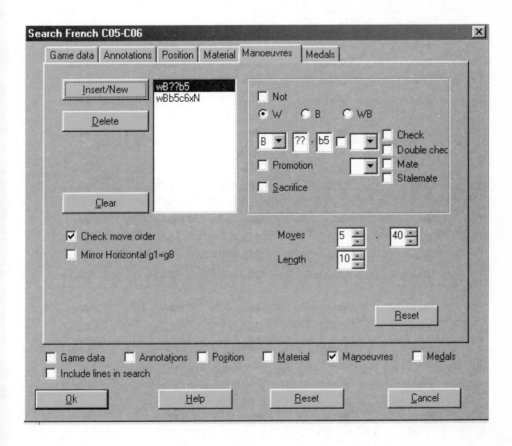

Figure 24

Filtering based on specific manoeuvres

This is very basic and very helpful. I then end up some 139 examples.
It is of course futile to go through all of these in order to determine
anything useful. I already have my own ideas about in which positions
this manoeuvre might be executed from the examples I have already
seen. So although I might end up with some different games, I quickly
find positions I feel are relevant – which are examples such as:

□ Lutz ■ R.Bagirov

Istanbul 2000

French Defence

It should be noted that this is not the ghost of the old Alekhine warrior Vladimir Bagirov who simply could not bear to miss the Olympiad, but a youngster, Rufat Bagirov, from Azerbaijan. The old Bagirov has sadly passed away, but like any true action hero he died at the board, according to rumours in a winning position. As Jack Nicholson said in the shape of the Joker in the first Batman film: If you got to go, go with a smile. The chess world is poorer place without the old Bagirov, let us hope the younger version will bring honour to the name. Not that it happens in this game...

18...Rac8 19 Bxc6 Rxc6 20 Rfc1 Rfc8 21 Rxc6 Rxc6 22 Nc3 Rc4 23 Rd1 h6 24 h3 a6 25 Rd2 b5 26 a3 Qg5 27 Qxg5 hxg5 28 f3 Be8

29 Nd1 Rc1 30 Kf2 Bg6 31 Ne3 Rb1 32 Ng4 Kf7 33 Ne5+ Kf6 34 Nd7+ Kf7 35 Nb8 a5 36 Nc6 a4 37 Na7 Rc1 38 Nxb5 Bc2 39 Nc7 Bb3 40 Na6 Rc8 41 Nc5 e5 42 Ke3 exd4+ 43 Kxd4 1-0

This might seem a quite naive example of positional chess to some, but I find these kinds of examples very useful. For some players this idea of exchanging the bishop for knight to gain a permanent advantage of knight vs. bishop might not be so evidently decisive as it appears when you go through the examples. But still, Grandmasters ended up in this situation with Black, and lost, or Grandmasters used this strategy to win games – depending on what side you choose to see it from.

In my search for Bb5xNc6 examples I also got the following less usual example, but still one I find telling about the positions in the French Tarrasch, and therefore choose to include in my new database **French Middlegames C05-C06.**

☐ Benjamin ■ Remlinger

Honolulu 1996

French Defence

---

1 e4 e6 2 d4 d5 3 Nd2 Nf6 4 e5 Nfd7 5 Bd3 c5 6 c3 Nc6 7 Ngf3 Qb6 8 0-0 g6 9 dxc5 Qc7

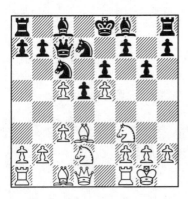

10 Bb5 Bg7 11 c4 0-0 12 cxd5 exd5 13 Nb3 a6 14 Bxc6 bxc6 15 Bf4 Nxe5 16 Bxe5 Bxe5 17 Nxe5 Qxe5 18 Qd2 Bd7 19 Rfe1 Qf6 20 Qd4 Qxd4 21 Nxd4 Rfb8 22 Re7 Rb4 23 Rd1 Re8 24 Rxe8+ Bxe8 25 b3 f6 26 Kf1 Bd7 27 Ke2 Kf7 28 Kd3 Rb8 29 Re1 g5 30 Kc3 h5 31 b4 h4 32 a3 Ra8 33 Kb3 a5 34 bxa5 Rxa5 35 Kb4 Ra8 36 a4 f5 37 a5 Kf6 38 Ra1 Ra6 39 Kc3 Bc8 40 Nc2 Ra8 41 Nb4 Ba6 42 Kd4 Bb5 43 a6 g4 44 Ra5 Kg5

45 Rxb5 cxb5 46 c6 f4 47 g3 fxg3 48 fxg3 h3 49 c7 1-0

Another theme that often arose was a black exchange sacrifice on f3. So I do the same again, choosing the manoeuvre ...Rxf3 and gxf3, as these were the times when the sacrifice seemed positionally justified.

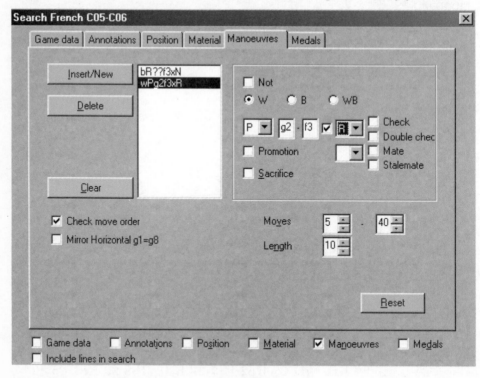

Figure 25

Searching by manoeuvre

This time it gave me 148 games. So I basically do the same thing: I play through the top 30-50 examples, depending on how deep I feel it is useful to go with the concept in question. A move like ...Rxf3!? naturally occurs in more concrete circumstances than Bb5xNc6 and it is less easy to say something definite about the examples. Here a thorough analysis could be useful. Pick maybe ten games that look especially interesting and study them carefully. Not the endgames, nor the opening, but the positions around the exchange sacrifice. You will then learn a lot about this specific concept in the French, and be able to write down your conclusions in your database. I am a great fan of this procedure, as it helps me remember things better. First of all memory works better on something concrete, as it basically works with images. Secondly, I know for sure that I have a conclusion. And finally, rereading my conclusion will help prompt my memory, and make me recall my thoughts and feelings.

Here is a good example of the exchange sacrifice on f3 in its most triumphant form.

□ **Hebden** ■ **Gleizerov**
Port Erin 2001
French Defence

1 e4 e6 2 d4 d5 3 Nd2 Nf6 4 e5 Nfd7 5 Bd3 c5 6 c3 Nc6 7 Ne2 cxd4 8 cxd4 f6 9 exf6 Nxf6 10 0-0 Bd6 11 Nf3 0-0 12 Bf4 Bxf4 13 Nxf4 Ne4 14 Ne2

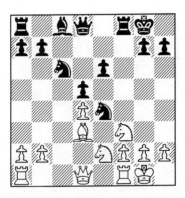

In this position the sacrifice is the theoretical main line. But 17 Qb3?! is a new try.

14...Rxf3 15 gxf3 Ng5 16 Kh1 e5 17 Qb3 Kh8 18 Bb5 e4 19 fxe4 dxe4 20 Qg3 Nf3 21 Bxc6 bxc6 22 Rfd1 Be6 23 Ng1 Nh4 24 h3 Bd5 25 Kh2 Qf6 26 Rd2 Rf8

27 Rc2 Nf5 28 Qf4 Qe7 29 Qe5 Qh4 30 Rf1 Nxd4 31 Rd2 Nf3+ 32 Nxf3 Rxf3 33 Qe8+ Bg8 34 Qd7 e3 35 Re2 Qf4+ 36 Kg1 h6 37 b3 Bd5 38 Qg4 exf2+ 39 Rfxf2 Rg3+ 40 Kf1 Rxg4 0-1

The search for manoeuvres in this kind of position can have a wide range of course, and material search can have a great relevance in middlegame positions as well. You can, for instance, search for opposite-coloured bishops, or one bishop and one knight each, which is a fairly common material division in this line. It is what you notice when you first go through the games that decides what you choose to look at later.

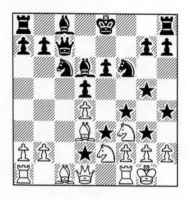

White plans Bc1-g5-h4-g3

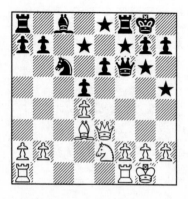

Black plans Bc8-d7-e8-h5

There is an obvious drawback to this kind of analysis that you should be aware of. If a manoeuvre like ...Bc8-h5 is good, you will often find it prevented in games between strong players. But then, when you use ChessBase to search for the manoeuvre, you will naturally not get the examples where the manoeuvre has been prevented! In the diagram above one could imagine that apart from 17...Bd7 (as played in the game) 17...a6!? also makes good sense, as White probably should have replied to 17...Bd7 with 18 Bb5! creating pressure. Then again Black should reply 18 Bb5 with 18...Nb8! avoiding the possible unfavourable situation with bishop against knight, as described above.

It is my firm conviction that using the method of database analysis you are much better prepared for your games than with any other method of opening preparation – even memorising long and complicated lines. Of course this is always a matter of which openings you play but, as illustrated with the two earlier examples from the Sveshnikov, most people these days are pragmatic in their choice of openings. Positional understanding has become an even stronger tool in the computer age, as it is now very dangerous to try to win the game right out of the opening against a decently-prepared opponent.

Specific Opening Analysis

But should the opponent walk into those few positions, which are hard to understand by general principles, then you had better be prepared. Let us look at one of my games to show how my opponent was one step in front of me, not to say one hundred steps!

□ **Aagaard** ■ **Gleizerov**
Hoogeveen 2000
French Defence

1 e4 e6 2 d4 d5 3 Nd2 Nf6 4 e5 Nfd7 5 c3 c5 6 Bd3 Nc6 7 Ne2 cxd4 8 cxd4 f6 9 exf6 Nxf6 10 Nf3 Bd6 11 0-0 Qc7 12 Bg5 0-0 13 Bh4 Nh5 14 Qc2 h6 15 Bg6 Rxf3 16 gxf3 Bxh2+ 17 Kh1 Nf4 18 Ng3 Qb6 19 Rad1 Nxd4 20 Rxd4 Qxd4 21 Bh7+ Kh8 22 Kxh2 g5 23 Qc7 Qg7 0-1

Not a very successful game from my side to say the least, but quite illustrative concerning opening preparation. But let us assume that I am not me, and I just study the French. If I was to play Gleizerov the next day I would maybe speculate whether or not I wanted to enter such a dangerous line. But this is not currently my concern. Now I am at home with time on my hands, wanting to understand this line better. Let us pretend that I was not the first player to meet 18...Qb6, that I saw this annoying game where White lost horribly, but still wanted to play the line because it looks good for White otherwise.

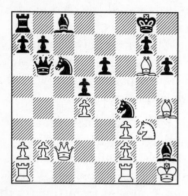

position after 18...Qb6!

I would most likely start by making a search after 18 Ng3 to see if there are more pitfalls I should know about. After the search I collect all the games and **Merge** them (see Figure 26).

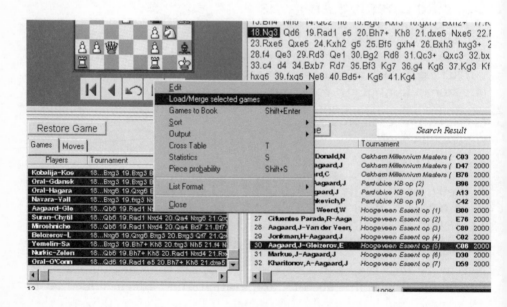

Figure 26

Merging relevant games

This basically means I collate all the games in a single main game, albeit in a rather random order. After this I choose **Reorder variations** (Figure 27) to get the games organised. ChessBase is not perfect for reordering the variations, but it is close enough to be an excellent tool. (One small mistake arising from Reordering is that the previous 'main game' is sometimes sent into the sub-lines, with no text attached to it. So when you find a game with no player information appended, it is your main game.).

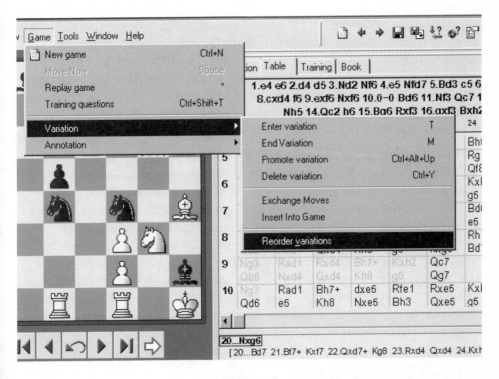

Figure 27

Reordering the variations

Having done this I now have a good starting point towards a full overview of what other people have played in this position. Often you can find important evaluations and analysis in opening books, but these days you just as often find the evaluation of variations change faster than publishers are able to keep up with. Opening books therefore have slightly different roles these days. They are no longer a source for all the newest games, even though we expect the writer to be as up-to-date as possible. Rather, opening books these days are collected wisdom and guides into the core of an opening, as well as structured information and theoretical overview. I personally use the Encyclo-paedias from *Informant* in my opening preparations. Not because I trust the evaluations and annotations I find in them, but because they are the opening books with the best structure and most information. They tell me what I should look out for, and what I might not have realised when I went through my database.

After organising the games it becomes apparent to me that no anti-dote has been found to 18...Qb6 so far, even though no strong player played it in 2001 – for that there can be many reasons. So far it seems that Black is just a lot better here. I then turn to Fritz for advice. This is the perfect situation for getting help from a chess playing program, as the situation has little strategic depth. Usually computers are of great help in analysing highly tactical situations, although I strongly encourage all my students first to try and find the moves by them-selves. If the computer thinks for you in the home, then you will miss it when you sit at the board.

So here I would take the position to Fritz and let it have some time to think things over. Not because I trust the computer to work by itself, but because I need a break anyway. When I return one hour later Fritz has some suggestions to make, but little faith in the white posi-tion. Here it should be obvious to everyone that a deeper look is needed. The combination of human intuition and the computer's abil-ity to see more moves in one second that we do over a lifetime is very useful. (If Deep Fritz calculates more moves in one second that Kram-nik will do over his lifetime, then why are they equals? Simply be-cause the computer calculates so much garbage that Kramnik has learned to disregard).

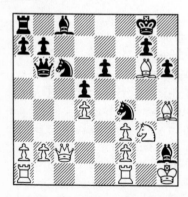

position after 18...Qb6!?

So I simply move the pieces around and try out all kinds of variations, even if Fritz insists that I am being ridiculous. Sometimes it changes its mind, sometimes I have just found another way that does not work. Eventually I will know enough to draw a valid conclusion. In this position my conclusion is that Black is better. I simply cannot not find a move for White to keep the ship afloat. 19 Rac1!? looked good at first, but after 19...Bd7 20 Kxh2 Nxd4 21 Bh7+ Kh8 22 Qc7 Qxc7 (22...Nxf3+ 23 Kh1 Nxh4? 24 Qxf4!) 23 Rxc7 Bc6! White is lost.

An important point is that Fritz is certain that the position after 23...Nxf3+ 24 Kh1 Kxh7 25 Rxd7 Nxh4 26 Rc1 is winning for Black, but the compensation established by the white rooks on the seventh rank is severe. So it looks as if White has no safe path through all these problems and that 18...Qb6!? is a brilliant novelty by my opponent, which has sandbagged the whole line for White. Well at least it did to me. Others have the power to merge high originality and the will to go places where the computer cannot. The following game shows the most recent battle in this variation.

☐ **Iuldachev** ■ **Gleizerov**
Abu Dhabi 2002
French Defence

1 e4 e6 2 d4 d5 3 Nd2 Nf6 4 e5 Nfd7 5 Bd3 c5 6 c3 Nc6 7 Ne2 cxd4 8 cxd4 f6 9 exf6 Nxf6 10 Nf3 Bd6 11 0-0 Qc7 12 Bg5 0-0 13 Bh4 Nh5 14 Qc2 h6 15 Bg6 Rxf3 16 gxf3 Bxh2+ 17 Kh1 Nf4 18 Ng3 Qb6 19 Rad1 Nxd4 20 Qa4!

This is the improvement. White is using his lead in development to attack. As White invests a serious amount of material in the process, programs are not capable of foreseeing the coming fireworks.

20...Nxg6?!

In Miroschnichenko - Borovikov, Ukraine 2001 Black played 20...Bd7, which seems more natural. But after 21 Bf7+ Kxf7 22 Qxd7 Kg8, GM Magomedov comes up with the following in *Informant 86* to prove that this is also not playable. White continues 23 Bf6!! gxf6 24 Rg1 Bxg1 (24...Kh8 25 Ne4) 25 Rxg1 Kf8 26 Ne4 and wins. Black cannot bale out with 22...Ke7 in this line, as 23 Be7+ Kg8 24 Bf6 just transposes.

21 Qe8+!

A very anti-chip idea. After 21 Qxd4 Qxd4 22 Rxd4 Bxg3 23 Bxg3 Bd7 Black stood well in Suran-Chytilek, Czech Team Championship 2000.

21...Kh7?

Magomedov again finds what the computer cannot. After the tougher defence 21...Nf8 he gives the following line: 22 Nh5!! (With the idea Nf6+) 22...Be5 23 Be7 Nf5 24 Qf8 Kh7 25 f4! Qc7 26 fxe5 Qxe7 27

Qxe7 Nxe7 28 Rd4! with a very clear edge, as Black cannot develop freely: 28...Bd7 29 Rg4 Nf5 30 Rg1 and White wins.

22 Nh5!

22...Be5

22...Nxh4 23 Nf6+! gxf6 24 Rg1! Bxg1 25 Rxg1 22...Nf5 23 Nf6+! gxf6 24 Qf7+ Ng7 25 Rg1! Qc7 26 Qxg6+ Kg8 27 Bxf6 both win (Notkin).

23 Rg1! Nf4

If 23...Nf5 24 Qxg6+ Kg8 25 Bf6! Qxf2 26 Bxe5 Qxf3+ 27 Rg2! Qxd1+ 28 Kh2 Notkin.

24 Nxf4 Nxf3 25 Ng6! Qc6 26 Qh8 1-0

A fantastic destruction of 18...Qb6!?, which we know now can be given a ? or ?!. It should be noted that **19 Nh5 Nxh5 20 Bxh5 Qxd4 21 Qg6!? Bd7! 22 Qf7+ Kh8 23 Bg3 Bxg3 24 fxg3 Ne5 25 Qe7**

with an unclear position has also been played – in the same tournament, only earlier. The game was Iuldashev-Bagirov, Abu Dhabi 2002.

This clearly shows how computers can aid us in opening analysis, but cannot find the way for us. Gleizerov might have gone through his novelty at home with his computer, but he did not really try to refute the black set-up, and therefore did not come up with all these sacrifices. The game above is presumably 100% home preparation.

Computers generally have a big problem understanding compensation. Shirov once said that when he started playing chess he realised that computers would have a huge impact on the way it would be played in the future, and he therefore tried to create a style where the computers would not understand what he was doing.

A very famous example of a novelty Fritz cannot understand is the following game:

□ **Aseev** ■ **Ivanov**
St. Petersburg 1997
Semi-Slav Defence

1 d4 d5 2 c4 e6 3 Nf3 Nf6 4 Nc3 c6 5 Bg5 dxc4 6 e4 b5 7 e5 h6 8 Bh4 g5 9 Nxg5 hxg5 10 Bxg5 Nbd7 11 exf6 Bb7 12 g3 c5 13 d5 Qb6 14 Bg2 b4 15 0-0 0-0-0 16 Na4 Qb5 17 a3 exd5 18 axb4 d4 19 Bxb7+ Kxb7 20 Nc3 dxc3 21 Qd5+ Kb6 22 Bf4

I remember back in 1993 when two of my friends, both strong IMs at the time, were playing this line at blitz with me watching. Around here one of them started thinking. They had analysed the line for hours together and had come to the conclusion that White was winning. Years later, after this game had travelled the globe, I confronted one of them with it, and with laughter he admitted that about this move *he simply had not given a thought.* Trust me, Fritz does not overlook anything, but it has no feelings and no power of evaluation. The game continued.

22...Rh5!!

The only move. Black loses after all the alternatives, e.g. 22...a6 23 Ra5 Qxb4 24 Rxa6+ Kxa6 25 Ra1+ Kb5 26 Bc7! and White has a winning attack, or 22...cxb2 23 Ra5 Qxb4 24 Bc7+! with mate to follow.

23 Qxh5 cxb2 24 Rad1

24...cxb4!!

The idea of the second rook sacrifice is all too much for the computer. Here the numbers start to go heavily in favour of White.

25 Bc7+ Kc6 26 Qxb5+ Kxb5 27 Bxd8 c3 28 Rxd7 a5

29 Rd5+

29 Rc7!? was probably what made people and computers later change to 28...c2. It is not my intention to go too deep into this game, rather to show a position where the computer cannot recognise the insignificance of two extra rooks in the fight against the four passed pawns.

29...Kc4 30 Rxa5 c2 31 Be7 b1Q 32 Bxf8 Qxf1+ 33 Kxf1 c1Q+ 34 Kg2 Qb1 35 Ra4 Qe4+ 36 Kg1 Qe1+ 37 Kg2 Qe4+ ½-½

In this way Fritz can be very limited. Despite its great power of calculation it has no real imagination and its strategical understanding is based on algorithms. Quite complex algorithms of course, but still it is only a program. So one should not trust the mighty Fritz too much. Here is a situation that I find very amusing.

□ **Aagaard** ■ **Kempinski**
Holland 1998

In this position it takes Fritz 7 about 10 seconds to see that 50 Rh8!! would have won on the spot. (As this is a book on chess software I recommend you do one of two things: Either work out yourself why it is winning, and why there is no alternative way, or ask your computer!).

But back then it took Fritz 5 38 minutes to work it out. And when I fed the move to the machine, in no way did it understand the glory of it. As so often the proof of the pudding is in the eating. I asked the computer what it would play against it. The answer was the amusing 50...Rc2 51 Qh1 Rg2+ 52 Qxg2 and then 52...Kxh8. Let us look at the situation after 52 Qxg2 and try to compare the two diagrams.

Can you spot the main difference? Well, to a human the main difference is that the black rook has disappeared from the board. To Fritz the main difference was that the mate had vanished from the horizon, and the rook could now safely be taken. Of course this is not true. And after 38 minutes Fritz 5 realised it too.

But it is one thing to have little confidence in the computer's imagination and positional abilities, it is quite another to have too great belief in one's own tactical ability. I am sure it was not that which lead to my direct win in the opening against John in 1997. At this time computers were only starting to spread among us mortal players, and not everything was checked automatically. It so happens that I had looked at the line we played in the following game after Adams had published some annotations in *Informant*. At the time I wanted to see what Black should play, in my role as a second for a strong Danish player.

□ Aagaard ■ Emms

London 1997

Ruy Lopez

1 e4 e5 2 Nf3 Nc6 3 Bb5 a6 4 Ba4 Nf6 5 0-0 Bc5 6 Nxe5 Nxe5 7 d4 b5 8 Bb3 Bxd4 9 Qxd4 d6 10 f4 c5?!

This is probably not very good. Better is 10...Nc6.

11 Qc3 Neg4 12 e5 Ne4 13 Qf3 d5 14 c4 Nxh2!?

This move was suggested by Adams in his annotations. The following line is more or less forced.

15 Kxh2 Qh4+ 16 Kg1 Bg4 17 Qe3 Ng3 18 Re1 d4 19 Qd3 0-0 20 Nd2 Bf5 21 Qf3 Bg4 22 Qd3 Bf5

Here the annotations stopped with the evaluation *unclear*. We fed it into the computer and rejected it quite quickly because of the move played in the game.

Here John told me after the game that he had analysed some nice winning lines after 21 Qc6 and 21 Qb7, but the move I played in the game had simply evaded his eye. After this Black has no real way to save the game, though he can still put up a fight.

23 Ne4

Rather obvious, but somehow this was a blind spot for John.

23...Bxe4?

Here I later found the incredible 23...Nxe4 24 Rxe4 g5!!

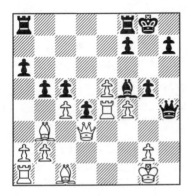

and only with the help of a computer program found a successful defence: 25 Bd2! Rab8 26 cxb5 axb5 27 e6 and White is winning. Of course I have not checked it since and I am dying to investigate it once more.

24 Rxe4 Qh1+ 25 Kf2 Nxe4+ 26 Qxe4 Rad8 27 Qe1 Qh4+ 28 Kf1 Qh1+ 29 Kf2 Qh4+ 30 g3 Qh2+ 31 Kf3 d3 32 Bd2 Rfe8 33 Qf2 Qh6 34 Kg2 Qb6 35 Rc1 b4 36 Ba4 Re6 37 Be3 f6 38 Bxc5 Qa5 39 Bb3 Kh8 40 Be3 fxe5 41 c5 Rf6 42 f5 Rdf8 43 g4 Qc7 44 Bd5 g6 45 Bg5 gxf5 46 Bxf6+ Rxf6 47 gxf5 Qd8 48 Be4 Rh6 49 Qg3 Qd4 50 Qxd3 Qxb2+ 51 Rc2 1-0

It must be said that I still believe quite a lot in finding the moves yourself first, and only then using the computer as a backup. In John's defence it should be said that the method of thinking for himself gave him a brilliant victory in this tournament with 7/9. All in all I think it is important to use computers only when we cannot do something ourselves. Opening preparation is one of these fields. We can come with new ideas and analyse collected material, but we cannot store all the games in our head, nor can we see every tactical possibility. Computers do not have blind spots, occasionally we do.

Bent Larsen once told me a very amusing story about computers. It was at the Sicilian Love tournament in Buenos Aires, I think, or a Najdorf Memorial tournament. Anand was giving Shirov a hard time because he only had 300,000 games in the database on his computer, when Ivanchuk came by.

'Chuky! Come here,' Anand said. Ivanchuk approached.

'How many games do you have in your database?'

'10,000.'

'10,000? Only 10,000?' Anand exclaimed.

'Yes,' Ivanchuk said with a voice divided between surprise and tears. 'I try and I try, but no matter what I do, I cannot remember more than 10,000 games.'

The story is of course polished for dramatic effect by Larsen. The real exchange was probably quite different.

Most modern database programs have some nice tools that can improve the work with openings. One function I particularly like in ChessBase is the **Repertoire printout**. I use it often when I want to work with my openings, but also want to get away from the computer. (My work in cognitive science gives me good reason to believe that working with actual chess pieces from time to time stimulates the mind. I also believe most analysis and discussion of variations should be performed in the head and not at the board. But this is to some extent speculation. In reality I just do what I feel most comfortable with.) This can be particularly useful for travelling, where going over your analysis might not be possibly in the plane, train or bus, if they are all confined to your laptop... or if you do not have a laptop (which of course is unheard of these days – you might not have a bike, a CD player, a TV or a bed, but of course you have a laptop!). Well, whatever excuse you want, it might be very handy to have your opening preparation in a printout that does not look like an extended representation of the number Pi. The way to use repertoire printout is to take your merged game, make sure it is in the best possible order, and then simply print it. The result could look like the following:

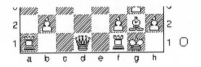

D44	1.d4 d5 2.Nf3 Nf6 3.c4 c6 4.Nc3 e6 5.Bg5 dxc4 6.e4 b5 7.e5 h6 8.Bh4 g5 9.Nxg5 hxg5 10.Bxg5 Nbd7 11.g3 Bb7 12.Bg2 Qb6 13.exf6 0-0-0 14.0-0 c5 15.d5 b4 16.Na4 Qb5 17.a3 exd5 18.axb4 d4

	19	20	21	22	23	24	25	26	27	28
1	bxc5	Nxc5	Qa4	Rfc1	Kxg2	Kg1	Rxc4	Rac1	Rxc5	Rxc5
	Nxc5	Bxc5	a6	Bxg2	Qb7+	Rdg8	Rxg5	Kb8	Rxc5	Qxb2[1]
2	Bxb7+	Nxc5	bxc5	f3	Rf2	Qxf3	Rf1	Rb1	Bf4	Rb8+[2]
	Qxb7	Bxc5	Ne5	Qxb2	Nxf3+	Qxa1+	Qa6	Rhe8	c3	
3	...	Re1	Qxd4	Qxc4	Nxb6	Qxf7+	Qe6+	Qf7+	Qe6+	Red1
	Kxb7	cxb4	Qxg5	Nb6	axb6	Kc6	Kb7	Kc6	Kb7	Rxd1+[3]
4	...	Bf4	Re1	b5	Re4	Nxb6	Re7+	Qf3+	Ra7+	Qxc6
	...	Qc6	d3	Qxb5	Nb6	axb6	Bxe7	Qc6	Kxa7	Bd6[4]
5	...	Nc3	Qd5+	Bf4	Qxh5	Rad1	Bc7+	Qxb5+	Bxd8	Rxd7
	...	dxc3	Kb6	Rh5	cxb2	cxb4	Kc6	Kxb5	c3	c2[5]
6	...	...	...	Ra5	bxc3	Rb1+	Rxb5+	Qxf7	Qd5[6]	Qf5
	...	...	...	Qxb4	Qxa5	Qb5	Kxb5	Bd6	Nb6	a5[7]

[1] **29.Qc6** Qb7 30.Qd6+ Ka8 31.Qxd4	Shanghai 2000/CBM 76 (29)
Re8 32.Qd5 Re1+ 33.Kg2 Re6 34.h4 Rxf6	

0%

Figure 28

The very useful repertoire printout

This way you can take your new opening analysis with you everywhere. If you have done your homework you will have a head start on your opponent that will often last way into the endgame. And you can take your homework with you and go through it from time to time. Either in the format of printouts or on your laptop. Or you can do like Chuky, and limit yourself to 10,000 games which are all in your head. Whatever you choose I feel comfortable that I have given you all the advice I can on using a computer for general opening preparation.

Chapter Five

General Training

The growth of general chess mastery has a far stronger influence on one's results than the improvement of one's opening understanding, because it will tell under the most diverse circumstances, in every stage of the battle, and not just in the opening of the game. – Mark Dvoretsky.

In this Chapter I will discuss some of the different ways you can use Fritz and ChessBase to improve your general playing level. Most people use chess playing programs for opening preparation and to replace their own work in analysing their own games, but very few have any idea how to use the programs to improve their general level. I hope to be able to give you some new ideas on how this is done.

How to train and how not to train with Fritz

Before turning to actual training methods, I would like to discuss the use and abuse of Fritz by many players. Fritz is a lovely tool, but at the end of the day it is a machine, and it cannot give us more back than we put into it. How many times have I not experienced the following situations?

A pupil tells me about a game he has played, where the next day the opponent comes running to ask about some position. What would you have played here? He then shows some variation that is completely bogus and finally says that Fritz thinks that here he is better. My pupil would then go a little back and show what he had intended. The opponent is baffled, even though this move is the only obvious one in the position, the move he had intended during the game. The opponent is baffled and in disbelief. This move certainly cannot be any good or else Fritz would have come up with it. He might then come back the next day with Fritz's suggestion against this line, and meet with the same kind of disbelief when my pupil continues to suggest other moves for himself than Fritz would have played.

In the end Fritz might be right or wrong. It is not so important. The important thing is that next time the two of them meet at the board, my pupil has the advantage of *having thought for himself first*. The most common mistake among chess players is *laziness*. They use the computer as a short cut to analysing their own games. But the things the computer tells them gives them no revelation, and their time is just as well spend watching TV or playing one-minute chess on the Internet Chess Club.

Another pupil recently told me that he would stop playing the Sicilian Dragon because Fritz consistently claimed that White was better no matter what line he was looking at. Again he did not really think himself. But OK, this is an 11-year old boy. The problem was easily solved by giving him a copy of Junior 7, which has a completely different opinion of the Dragon.

The mistake in both cases was that instead of using Fritz as a tool, it was used as an informer of truth. Computers are useful tools if we use them right, just as a knife is as useful tool. But if we do not know how to use it probably, we may cut our fingers. Fritz is a map, not the territory.

We can derive a lot of benefit from using Fritz to compensate us for the things we cannot do for ourselves. After we have analysed our own games extensively, we can take a last check with Fritz. If we really have looked carefully then Fritz will not be able to find obvious oversights, though this inevitably will happen from time to time. More importantly Fritz will come up with some ideas, which to the human eye will seem rather artificial. The best we can do then is to analyse them extensively for ourselves and then go back to the computer. Of course this is a question of time for many people, as much that as of discipline. We tend to be curious about our games and whether or not we have missed something, but we should direct this thirst for knowledge towards improving our game, and not just to quick answers of doubtful insight and value.

In my time in chess I have met only two kinds of player. The first category is the majority, who likes to play and also to talk a little about the game with the opponent afterwards. They do not really care about improving their play, they never buy books and only rarely use computers for chess, and if they do so, it is by playing blitz on the Internet. These people might occasionally give the impression that they want to play better, but it is just like me wishing I was good at playing the piano. I would love to, and I might even occasionally play a little on it. But I have never taken a formal lesson and most likely I never will. The second category is probably where you belong, as you are reading this book. This is people who want to do something to improve their game. It is my experience that most people use computers wrongly, because they are oblivious to the fact. We all cut corners from time to time, but few do so systematically once they are aware of how much they are wasting their time.

So let me say it clearly. It is better to analyse a game extensively by yourself, than to analyse 100 games with Fritz. Learn to think for yourself. There is no better path, and there will never be any better path. Not in chess, nor in anything else. To analyse with another human is even better, as you can share insights. Not moves. Insights, ideas. But still believe in yourself. And believe yourself.

Here are some ways to use Fritz and ChessBase meaningfully to improve your game.

Endgame training

The endgame is for most players the dark phase of the game where they feel quite lost and would love to have telepathic contact with Fritz or Ulf Andersson or, if they are not available, God. But serious study can turn this around and this does not have to mean memorising endless variations and positions in R+2 pawns against R+1 pawn. Previously there was a tendency for endgame study to be like this. The endgame books are thick and no one could decide what to study and what not to study. All that could be said for certain was that reading Mikhail Shereshevsky's fabulous book *Endgame Strategy* would certainly be a plus. Beyond that – nothing. But the old days are truly old and we now know exactly what to do. Or to be precise, we now have a proven path to follow.

In 2002 Mark Dvoretsky published the book *Die Endspiel Universität* in German and an English version is due out at the start of 2003. Probably the title will be the same – *The Endgame University*. In this remarkable work Dvoretsky has introduced a new system to endgame books. Small diagrams indicate that a position might be interesting, but not important to remember. The big diagrams (which are in a clear minority) indicate that these positions should be learned by heart. In such a complicated and diverse area as pawn endgames (including queen against pawn) there are fifty positions. In other areas far fewer.

The best way to improve one's technique, according to Dvoretsky, is to go through the book and solve the exercises, but only try to remember the big diagrams. For this there is a simple technique I have decided to call:

The Danielsen Method

The Danielsen method is really simple – and effective. The Danish Grandmaster Henrik Danielsen explained it to me some years back, after he had used it to gain a very deep insight into the endgame. He had simply entered a lot of theoretical positions into a database and then used it for repetition frequently. It is not the same as when you read a book and have a qualitative learning experience. Here you have a quantitative learning experience, which can be repeated frequently. Danielsen explained to me that this would help the brain to adapt patterns and later put them into use via an improved intuition. My work in cognitive science and my general common sense makes me believe that he is right. But the problem was that the work was simple exhausting. I did enter 800 positions from Averbakh's rook endgame books, but I never got any further. I had the same feeling as most people do when they read endgame books – are all these positions really relevant? In some ways within this method they *are* relevant, and in some ways not. I remember looking at an endgame with a strong player who explained that he, too, had studied the rook endgame book by Averbakh in its entirety, but he did not have any understanding of keeping the rook active or behind the pawns. So I think you need some combination of qualitative training – meaning reading good books – and repetition of the most important examples. And here the Danielsen method combined with the Dvoretsky book is close to ideal. There is of course some initial work to be done in entering all the big diagrams into a database, but this can de defined in hours not days, and the benefits last a lifetime.

This time I include all variations so I can go through them too more slowly from time to time, so that my brain does not grow immune to the ideas and meanings of the positions. Unfortunately, ChessBase 8.0 does not have the **Automatic replay** function of earlier Chess-Base programs. However, it is available in ChessBase 7.0. For those with only ChessBase 8.0 who would like to use this method, there is a solution. On www.chessbase.com it is possible to download a program called ChessBase Light free of charge. This program is a limited version of ChessBase 6, which does have this function. So the way it works is like this. You copy all the positions you want to work with to the clipboard and then press Ctrl+A to mark them all. Then you choose automatic replay as illustrated in Figure 29.

Figure 29

The automatic replay feature

The program then starts to play through the main lines of the positions. You can adjust the speed to your own liking. The only thing I dislike about this (now lost) function is that it makes the first move of the game instantly. It would be better if it took a pause first. At least it does so at the end.

For repetition this is quite a useful tool, as one easily becomes tired of using the fingers. And the great thing is that when you have marked all the games in the clipboard, it automatically continues with the next game. For some reason it does not do so if you have automatic replay directly from the database.

The following example is from my database of Dvoretsky endgames. 1-137 refers to the number in the Dvoretsky book (see Figure 30).

This is basically the Danielsen method and I highly recommend it – especially if you are not working alone, but have friends who can share the tiresome job of entering the positions to begin with. I do not think that this is a breach of copyright as you are not copying the original material – the exact choice of words and explanations in the book. And morally I see no problem either, as acquiring a file like this will only encourage a receiver to buy the book, especially when he sees what a great book it is.

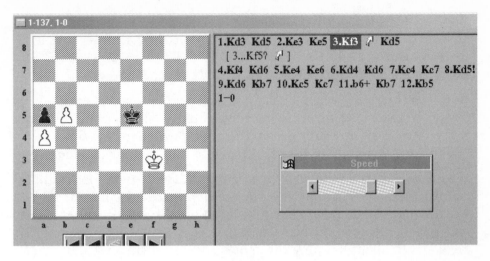

Figure 30

Automatic replay in action

Playing theoretically complex positions

When you go through a book like Dvoretsky's you will inevitably find many positions of theoretical value, which cannot be memorised. The reason is that they are fought on ideas and basic concepts rather than specific move orders. The following well-known endgame is typical:

□ **Dautov** ■ **Alterman**
Germany 1998

31 Rc7 Re2 32 Rxa7 h5 33 Kf3 Rc2 34 h4 Kg7 35 Ra6 Rb2 36 Ke3 Rc2 37 Ra4 Rb2 38 f3 Rc2 39 Ra6 Rb2 40 Ra8 Kf6 41 Ra4 Kg7 42 Ra6 Rc2 43 a4 Ra2 44 Ke4 Ra3 45 Ra8 Kf6 46 Ra6+ Kg7 47 a5

Ra4+ 48 Kd5 Ra3 49 Kc6 Rc3+ 50 Kb7 Ra3 51 f4 Ra1 52 Ra8 Kf6
53 a6 Kf5 54 Rf8 Rb1+ 55 Ka7 f6 56 Rb8 Re1 57 Rb3 Kg4 58 Kb6
Re6+ 59 Ka5 Re7 60 Ra3 g5 61 fxg5 fxg5 62 hxg5 Re5+ 63 Kb6
Rxg5 64 a7 Rg8 65 Rc3 Rg6+ 66 Kb7 Rg7+ 67 Kb8 1-0

It is always striking when a truly professional player such as GM Alterman – who wakes up every morning thinking 'What should I analyse
today?' – can lose an easily drawn theoretical endgame like this. And
lose in a way that makes it look as if White was winning all along.

What I do with my pupils at times is to let them defend these kind of
difficult endgames against the *Advanced Aagaard* – Aagaard and
Fritz in a nasty alliance. They have been taught the principles of the
endgame in advance of course, and then they get to apply them. It is
an old truth about learning that knowledge is quickly lost if it is not
useful in some way. This is certainly a way to make it useful. Also, it
can be hard to trust one's own understanding of these principles, if
one has not tried them out in practice.

Of course Fritz is not the most dangerous endgame player. It has
some problems understanding that a pawn can be worth the same as
a rook, and similar things – but it is still a pawn up here, and if you
defend no better than Alterman, I am certain that you will lose. Here
is my attempt at applying the principle of creating kingside counterplay as quickly as possible.

☐ **Fritz 7** ■ **Aagaard**
Copenhagen 2003

---

31 Rc7 Re2 32 Rxa7 h5 33 Kf3 Rb2 34 h4 Kg7 35 a4 Ra2 36 Ra6
f6 37 Ra7+ Kh6 38 a5 g5 39 Ra6 Kg6 40 hxg5 Kxg5 41 Ra8 Ra3+
42 Kg2 Ra2 43 a6 Kf5 44 Ra7 Ra4 45 Kf3 Ra3+ 46 Ke2 Ra2+ 47
Ke3 Ra3+ 48 Kd4 Ra2 49 Kc5 Rxf2 50 Re7 Kg4 51 Rg7+ Kf3 52 a7
Ra2 53 Kb6 f5 54 Kb7 f4 55 gxf4 Kxf4 56 Rh7 Kg4 57 a8Q Rxa8
58 Kxa8 h4 59 Ka7 h3 60 Kb6 Kg3 61 Kc6 h2 62 Kc5 Kg2 63 Rg7+
Kh1 64 Rd7 ½-½

A comfortable draw it seems, and the end is slightly bizarre. Fritz
sees that it cannot prevent the pawn from queening, and therefore can
see no reason to bring the king nearer. Not very testing, but I am sure
it would have made no difference.

The game was played with 4 minutes + 2 seconds per move. Even with
this rapid time control you can get a good feeling, and besides that of
knowing I could defend this endgame, an extra bonus was the

following position.

□ Fritz 7 ■ Aagaard

Copenhagen 2003

Here Fritz played the harmless 54 Kb7, but during the game I had doubts about the correctness of my play. What about 54 Rg5!? After the game had finished I went back and found a solution myself, as I should, and then tested it with Fritz, who said I was right. The test was actually only to strengthen my confidence, as I had no doubts it was correct. Still I think it is good to be 101% sure, and only a computer could give that extra little percent. Black should play:

54...Rb2+ 55 Kc7 Rc2+ 56 Kb7 Rb2+ 57 Ka8 Rb5!

White has no way to win this position. After a move like 58 Rg8 White will win the rook for the pawn, but after 58...f4 Black will draw in similar fashion to the game. The same goes for 58 Rxh5 Kxg3.

Suddenly I had something to think about, and the essence of the end-game is much more likely to stay fresh in my head.

Of course I need not to limit myself to theoretical endgames. Recently the German super-grandmaster Christopher Lutz published a book called *Endgame Secrets*. A fine little book with 45 analysed endgames (in my German edition). What you could do is to play these endgames against Fritz and then compare your results with the analysis in the book. Or you can take endgames from *Informant*, or other books. What I highly recommend you do is to take the positions from books *with strong analysis*. Do not think that Fritz will reflect on anything beyond its own limits. Remember, it is a machine.

Playing Studies against Fritz

One thing is to play positions with no accurate solution. Another is to solve complicated positions with only one correct path to victory. Sometimes I want to solve some really difficult positions, where I know for sure that I cannot see all the moves in advance. Or I want my students to do that. The best possible solution to this is to have a trainer going over the exercises with you. You put up the position and play against the book.

But oh, this chess writing is a tough business, and though my publishers are nice and fair, I cannot afford to have a full time trainer coming around whenever I want. So to make up for this I have some sessions with a friend. We both know a bit about collecting material and it is easy to play the moves from the book on the board. But again, he has a day job and I usually sleep at night, so we cannot get together so often. In this instance I use Fritz. I set up the study in Fritz and play it as a normal position. Here it is important to give Fritz some time to think about its moves, as otherwise it might not come up with the best possible defence, which is a shame. For study I would set the time for perhaps one hour each, and then whenever I grow tired waiting for the computer, I would just press the space bar.

When you do this kind of training it is of course important to turn off the computer's engine. Well, not actually turn it off, but just remove it from the screen, so that you do not get any hints in the process. This is done in the following way:

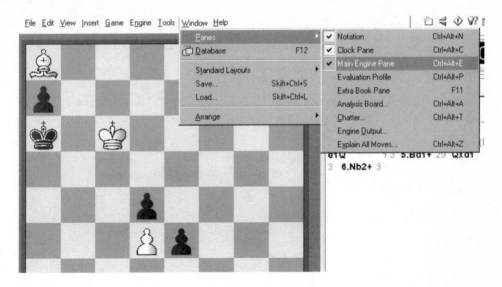

Figure 31

Hiding the computer engine

Below I have given two studies that I quite like and have tested with the computer. Of course you can find situations in which the computer does not give the best defence, since what the best defence is in practice against a human is not necessarily what the computer thinks is the best defence. I can only say that I have not found it to be a problem that the computer deviates from the solution in the book, as this normally happens only at the very end, when I have solved everything already.

<table>
<tr><td>Study 1</td><td>Study 2</td></tr>
</table>

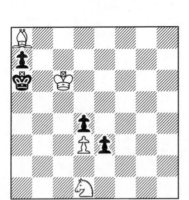

115

Solutions to studies

Study 1

This is a composition by V.Vlasenko 1970. Artur Yusupov showed it to the Danish National team at a training session. I quite like it.

1 Nb2! Ka5

1...e2 2 Nc4 and mate follows.

2 Kc5 e2 3 Nc4+ Ka4

3...Ka6 4 Kc6 and mate follows.

4 Bf3!

4...e1R

Fritz obviously has a sense of humour.

5 Bd1+ Rxd1 6 Nb2+ Kb3 7 Nxd1 a5

8 Kd5!

Not 8 Kxd4 a4 9 Nc3 a3 when White only has a draw after 10 Ne2!.

8...a4 9 Kxd4 a3 10 Nc3 Kb4 11 Na2+ Kb3 12 Nc1+ Kb4

13 Kd5!!

Again the only move to win.

13...Kb5

The original is 13...Kc3 14 d4 Kc2 15 Kc4 Kxc1 16 Kb3 and wins.

14 Na2 Kb6 15 Kc4 Kc7 16 Kb3 1-0

Study 2

Composition by Rinck, Basler Nachrichien 1925. White wins by dominating the knight and bishop:

1 Bc6+ Kh3 2 Bd7+ Kh4 3 Rd4+ Kh5 4 Be8+ Kh6 5 Rg4

5...Bf2

5...Be1 6 Kg8! Nf3 7 Rg6+ Kh5 8 Rg3+ and White wins.

6 Kg8 Nh3 7 Rg2 Bc5 8 Rg6+ Kh5 9 Rc6+ and White wins

As a trainer I have a different method I use with my pupils. It is inherent in the ChessBase program and can of course also be used among friends. It is very simple. You enter the exercises on the computer into a separate file, which you can then send to your pupils/friends by e-mail, and they can solve them directly on the screen. You can either send just the starting positions without moves, or use the **Training function** inherent in the program. You find it here if you right-click on the file and then ask for **Properties**. Then click on training and the following box shows up:

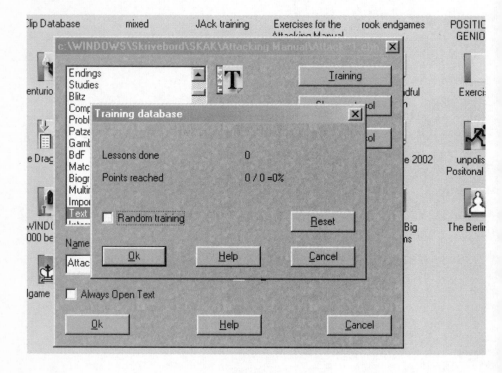

Figure 32

Using the training function

I highly recommend you click on the **Reset** button before sending it to anyone, as the **Points reached** should say 0/0 when you send the file to your pupil/friend. Otherwise the function might not work to your total satisfaction.

The positions will then appear on the screen in the following fashion:

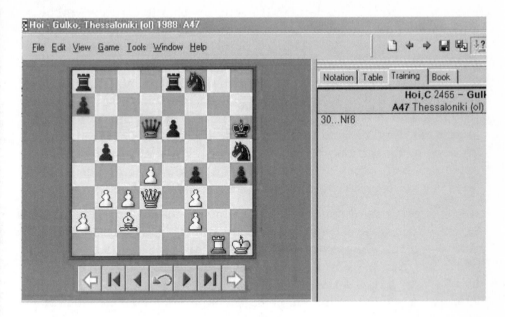

Figure 33

Let the training begin!

The only thing shown is the last played move and any annotations that might be attached to it. Then only the imagination sets limits on the ways to exploit this training option.

Middlegame Training

Of course computers can also be used to improve your calculation and middlegame strength. It might seem that this is the most obvious way to use the computer for training. In the Russian Chess School solving fixed exercises and setting up complex positions on the board, thinking about them, and then comparing your solutions with the original annotations, is the most common way to improve. It has best been described in the works of Alexander Kotov and Mark Dvoretsky, the two greatest Russian chess teachers known to the west.

What I suggest that you do is take some positions which are deeply complicated, set the clock for 15 or 20 minutes, and take good time to work out what is going on. After this you enter everything you have seen into ChessBase and go over your own analysis first with your own eyes. Then take the *advanced you* (you + computer) and go through the lines again to see if there was anything you missed. Being human, you should not feel bad if there was, but very happy if there was not. When I do this kind of training I normally use material by authors who write a lot of text in their notes. Books I can warmly recommend are: Igor Stohl's fabulous *Instructive Modern Chess Masterpieces*, John Nunn's two game collections and his book *Understanding Chess Move by Move*, as well as my own editor Byron Jacobs' fine little book *Analyse to Win*, which has very good examples for calculation training. The important thing about having text together with analysis, is that humans tend to think in concepts and ideas, and use a great deal of intuition in their calculations. For that reason textual explanation of concepts and ideas is a great supplement to the cold facts you get from Fritz and books like the *Sahovski Informant*.

Another very useful middlegame training technique is to play attacking or defensive positions against Fritz and afterwards analyse the games and see what you missed. Fritz has truly revolutionised the art of defence, and thereby also asked for higher technical performances by attacking players. GM Sune Berg Hansen, who generally is right in everything, said that the real change computers have made is in the minds of humans. Before we would not grab material because the opponent's compensation looked dangerous, but now we want to see the evidence before we reject the booty. Recently, World Champion Kramnik suffered a defeat in his match in Bahrain against Deep Fritz, as he had not seen a great defensive resource. When he approached it, the resource became apparent to him, so he chose another path, also leading to defeat – or did it? The following position could have arisen if Kramnik had chosen to play 27 Qe6+ Nf6 28 f4 instead of 27 Qh4+.

Black to move.

Here Fritz would have had only one way to keep the position closed to White's pieces: 28...Bh4!! and White will soon lose. One line is 29 gxh4 c3 and White has little to show against the two marching pawns. 29...Qg8+ should also win.

But just like Kasparov some years ago against Deep Blue, Kramnik resigned too early in this game. Michael Greengard, known as Mig on the Internet, found the following solution to White's worries:

□ Kramnik ■ Deep Fritz
Brains in Bahrain 2002

Here White should have continued to fight with 35 Rxa6 b2 36 Ra7+ Kg6 37 Rd7!! Rc1 38 Rd6+! Nf6 39 Rdd1 b1Q 40 Rxc1 Qf5 41 Rc6 as analysis with Fritz suggests that it would play something along the lines of 41...b5 42 Rb6 h5 43 Ree6 b4

44 Rxf6+! Qxf6 45 Rxb4

when there is no way for Black to break into the white fortress. Fortresses are a kind of defence that computers still struggle to understand. But beyond that, they are great defenders and can be used for pinning down attacks. I suggest that you take very promising positions from the books of Alekhine, Tal or Kasparov, or even better have a friend or a trainer pick some positions for you. Once again it is the comparison with the players' original annotations that will really make you wiser afterwards.

All of these methods of course include a computer and a chess playing program of some strength. But I think it is almost as important to have a friend with similar ambitions, or a trainer of some sort to help you, in order to make progress in chess. Not only because of the exchange of good training material for these kinds of exercises, but also because of the support you can get from someone who really believes in what you are doing. Personally I know no better way to motivate myself than to work with others. So find a friend with similar ambitions and convince him of the use you can be to each other.

Chapter Six

Special Computer Products

As well as database and actual playing programs there is also a variety of software products on the market for training and opening preparation, which are not unlike books. These CDs usually target tactics, positional or strategical training, if not at opening preparation. The tactics CDs have a different quality. One CD, *Intensive Tactics Course* by George Renko, is clearly aimed at not very strong players, as one of the most difficult problems on the first part (of two) of the CD is the following.

□ **Czerniak** ■ **Saharovsky**
Tel Aviv 1963

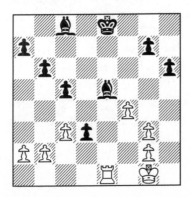

Black wins after 1...d2! 2 Rxe5+ Be6! 3 Rxe6+ Kd7. Not really a difficult exercise. Slightly harder is the following:

☐ Ionov ■ Zheinin
USSR 1980

White wins after the attractive little combination 1 Rxg5! Nxg5 2 Bxf6! gxf6 3 Qh8+ Kf7 4 Rh7+ and the queen is won. This is still not a very hard exercise compared with some completely wild books like *The Anthology of Chess Combinations* from Sahovski, which is probably my favourite book on combinations. For players who have just started looking at chess this kind of CD can be of great help, but usually some more advanced problems are needed. There are good CDs on tactics out there from both ChessBase and Chess Assistant and they are definitely worth your money. They have the advantage that you cannot accidentally see the solution to the next exercise – a fault with books I wanted solved for years and years.

One such product on the market is CT-ART 3.0, a tactics program recommended highly by Michael de la Maza in his groundbreaking *Rapid Chess Improvement*. CT-ART 3.0 has over 1,200 puzzles, most of which are meant for novices and intermediate chess players. However, there are also quite a few puzzles which would test even Grandmasters. If the user is struggling with an exercise, the program will offer certain hints, including using an auxiliary position on a 5x5 board to illustrate the main tactic in a more simplified form (see Figure 34 – the solution to both puzzles is ...Rg2!).

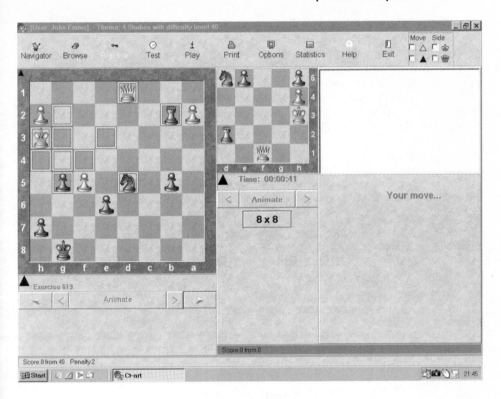

Figure 34

CT-ART 3.0 in action

Another genre is represented by a CD like Bartashinikov's *The Basic Principles of Chess Strategy 1-3*. This is not a collection of puzzles, but instructional books on a CD. They begin with text files explaining in abstract terms (see Figure 35) what is later illustrated in around 60 deeply annotated illustrative games. This is not very different from reading a book with a chessboard in front of you, and should be evaluated as such. The genre is fully valid and the CDs from Bartashinikov look acceptable. *Chess Assistant* has similar products available.

A third genre, one more suited to the computer, is opening CDs. The authors of these CDs compile all available material on a variation and then treat it as they like. A CD from Martin Breutigam on the *King's Indian with h3* seems to have taken full advantage of the computer's possibilities. First of all there is a database with more than 10,000 games played in the h3 line – the main position arises after 1 d4 Nf6 2 c4 g6 3 Nc3 Bg7 4 e4 d6 5 Nf3 0-0 6 h3. Secondly the author has created a Tree-file so you can manoeuvre around among the games and see what moves were played in what positions (see Figure 36).

Undermining the centre

If you have decided to concede the centre thus realizing the second strategy, you have to bear
following in mind: it is not advisable to concede the centre for a long time as then the struggl
it will become more difficult (if possible at all). Also it would be better if you think of your
undermining actions before. Which methods do you have for the undermining?

1. Pawn undermining the centre.

hessBase 8.0

Figure 35

CT-ART 3.0 in action

It is with functions like this that the CDs move towards being a real
alternative to books, for the reader as well as for the writer.

The third file is more in the way of a traditional book. The writer explains the different motifs and ideas, as well as structuring the variations. After this comes a lot of annotated Grandmaster games. Most of
them annotated by the author, but some also by people like Hazai,
Huzman and other annotators connected to ChessBase. A great advantage here over the traditional book is that whenever the author
explains a concept, he can make an internal link to games which illustrate what he is taking about (see the green link on Figure 37).

The fourth and final file on Breutigam's CD is a training file with a lot
of questions and answers. This is a very well-suited tool for repetition
of the previous file, and again demonstrates the potential of the computer. (see Figure 38).

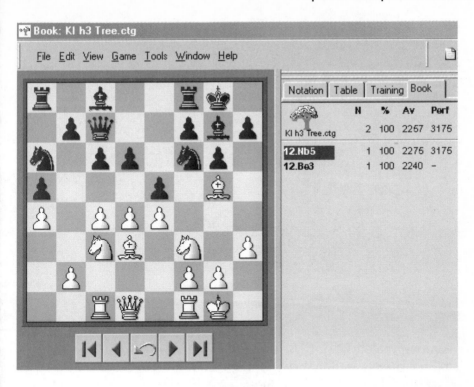

Figure 36

A tree file

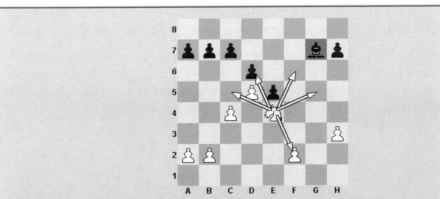

... on e4 the knight blocks Black's e-pawn, thus restricting the power of the bishop supporting White's plans on the g-file. A sqaure of one's dreams! Please note, that e4 not only hits forward, but also protects the vulnerable point f2.

In Kavalek,L - Torre,E 1-0 Black tried to take control ove the e4-square by sacrifici However, this mistaken tactical idea was punished with a good positional answer.

Figure 37

A useful link

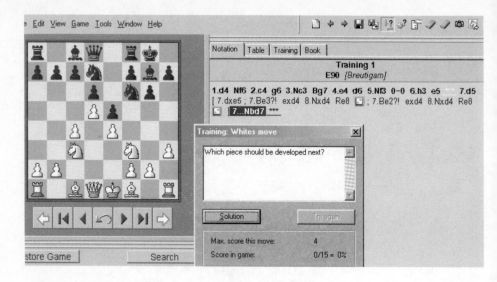

Figure 38

A tree file

The main problem with CDs from the publishers' point of view, and also the writers', is that they are installed a million times for every sold copy, and that sales therefore do not necessarily reflect the popularity of the CD, but do affect the payment to the writer. I fear that we will not see many great products in this genre, which we might had the CD burner not been invented, or had the programmers found a better and cheaper way to protect products against this abuse.

As it is now, most CDs seem very expensive in order to compensate for the loss by multiple copying, but I doubt that sales would go up markedly if the price went down, so it is easy to understand the producers' high prices.